Get Lost!

Adventure Tours in the Owyhee Desert

By Steve Silva

authorHOUSE®

AuthorHouse™
1663 Liberty Drive, Suite 200
Bloomington, IN 47403
www.authorhouse.com
Phone: 1-800-839-8640

First published by AuthorHouse 12/18/2008

ISBN: 978-1-4343-7069-3 (sc)

Library of Congress Control Number: 2008911285

Printed in the United States of America
Bloomington, Indiana

This book is printed on acid-free paper.

Maps created with TOPO! software
© 2006 National Geographic Maps.
To learn more visit:
http://www.nationalgeographic.com/topo

Contents

Chapter 1

Introduction

Eastern Oregon, Southwest Idaho and Northern Nevada represent some of the most remote riding possibilities in all of the lower contiguous United States. Comprised of mainly high altitude desert, or steppes, this area of interest is one of the largest tracts of unimproved land in the lower 48. Bordered by the Snake River Plain to the east, the Jarbidge Mountains to the south, and the Owyhee River canyons to the west. This area is host to dry arid sagebrush, jagged granite spires, dark canyons, volcanic lava beds, juniper forests, and a stillness that has led many to call it "The Big Quiet". Not for the faint of heart, this land has had settlers, immigrants, and historical implications for hundreds of years. Their marks are still here for all to see.

Dual sport motorcycles, adventure riding, or whatever tag you put on it has opened up a whole new array of access to this wild and lonely land. With only the availability of fuel to restrict the range of discovery, the average rider can enjoy this vast land and all it has to offer.

The area is crisscrossed with old roads and trails ranging from maintained gravel roads at the high end of use, to faint double tracks that are whispers of a direction at the seldom-used end. Terrain includes spectacular vistas, flat "tables", deep shadowed canyons, and tree lined mountaintops. Wildlife abounds, with deer, antelope, and coyotes howling in the starlit night skies. Constantly changing, the area offers a fantastic choice for the rider to enjoy, and explore. With the burgeoning group of dual sport riders, bikes, equipment, and technical mapping info, the adventure rider now has at his fingertips this entire region to enjoy.

Until now, most information concerning this enormous desert country was confined to a few obscure local guidebooks, mainly with an emphasis on hunting or historical significance. A handful of self proclaimed desert rats, ranchers and other family based individuals have also jotted down their histories and observations. But there has never been any reliable information on riding into the true backcountry of this immense desert land.

My intent is to put this information into a usable format that will enhance the opportunities in the area, without providing a by the numbers experience. Trust me, there is nothing static here. For as much as time has rendered and shaped these desert vistas, the land is dynamic and ever changing.

There will be much information that is purposely left out of this guidebook. It is just that, a guide. Take the lead and follow your own paths. I am just helping to smooth out some of the initial steps. Man has wandered this area for thousands of years, and it is not my intention to make this a follow the trail type of experience. I am sure that many users will be frustrated with the guides' shortcomings, as well as others who feel that too much information has been provided. Again, my intent is to provide a well-rounded overview, and leave the details to you, the rider, to fill in the gaps and to engage in your own relationship with this wild and open land.

History has left a legacy of lonely cabins, overgrown canyons, meandering sand washes, and cool trickling springs. Mining, ranching, and farming; these are the foundations of the area, both past and present. These individuals, usually generations of the same family, continue to carve out a quiet, sometimes desperate existence by today's standards, but revel in the quality of their deep-seated lifestyles.

As we ride through this amazing land, we see signs everywhere of the ongoing battle between the new, the old, and the almost forgotten. So go forth, ride, enjoy, and take a moment to think about those that have come and gone before us as you travel and explore this wild desert land. Your experience will be your own, and you should take ownership of it. The desert is a very special place, sometimes intense, sometimes vague, sometimes emotional, sometimes physical, and sometimes even spiritual. One thing you can count on is that it will always be different. I hope that you enjoy all of your experiences. Be safe.

The wide-open view from the cockpit.

Chapter 2

History, Past and Present

The southwest corner of Idaho is a hidden gem filled with natural wonders. Well, maybe not quite so hidden any longer. The Snake River Plain is a broad swath of geological matter made up of primarily rhyolite and basalt types of mineral composition. Throw in some granite outcroppings courtesy of the Idaho Batholith and you have one wild landscape. The rhyolite is the product of a long row of forgotten and now extinct volcanoes from around 13 million years ago. The rhyolite that covers most of the granite was from eruptions caused by a meteorite impact 17 million years ago. The granite and mineralization that followed has led to extensive mining and these discoveries are what eventually led to the present populations in the area, and to the gold and silver discoveries for which the Owyhee and much of Idaho in general are now famous for.

The Snake River Plain is also famous for one of the most incredible natural events in history, the Great Bonneville Flood. In a previous ice age, the Great Salt Lake was as large as today's Great Lakes. The water finally rose to a point where it overflowed through the Red Rock Pass near the southern border of Idaho, and emptied into the Snake River Plain drainage. The ensuing flood filled the entire Snake River Canyon above and beyond its brim, and then continued to surge across the Snake River Plain! It tore apart basalt cliffs, ripped boulders and scoured all the loose rock and gravel in its path, finally depositing them in groups as the impetus slacked and the waters lowered. Melon gravel bars dot the canyon, formed by the banging and dragging of basalt rocks against each other in the rushing water and current. These piles of melon shaped rocks can be seen along Highway 78, and are well known for being prime locations for Native American rock art. The sheer volume of water released from the flood has been calculated at close to one third of a cubic mile per hour – or about three times the size of the discharge of the Amazon River. Geologists claim that if you could have been around to watch the action, you would have been able to hear loud booming as the rocks under the water banged and rolled over and against one another! One of the greatest floods ever recorded, it may have only lasted at best a few months. The results though are still with us, complete with visual evidence as we ride and explore the area.

Lying within the Owyhee River drainage, the Owyhee country is graced by a mixture of flat plateaus cut and scarred by canyons. It ranges in elevations from 2000 feet above sea level along the Snake River Plain, to a high point of just over 8400 feet atop Hayden peak, which sits above the famous ghost town of Silver City. The riding season is long with only the true wetness of spring thaw, and the high elevation snow pack stopping specific areas of riding.

Temperatures range from below zero with frigid and extreme cold during winter, to sizzling 100 degree-days in the heat of summer. It is very normal for a day to begin with a cool and bracing 40 degree morning, and warm up to triple digit afternoons. The desert is an example of extreme in all its glory. The air is dry and relative humidity light. Rainfall consists of spring showers, and winter snows at higher elevations. Annual moisture is only 10-14 inches, mostly accumulated in the spring months.

Generally speaking, plants of the desert are Big Sagebrush, cheatgrass, and shadscale. Rabbit brush, Juniper, and Mountain Mahogany grow at higher elevations. Stands of Aspen and some cottonwood and poplar are common around predictable and sustained water sources, mainly creek bottoms and springs. The old Basque sheepherders' initials are often times carved into the white skin and can still be read to this day. But by and large, the Sagebrush is lord over this domain, its aroma and sheer size evidence of the long years of habitation. Wildflowers are abundant as the spring wetness comes on. Indian paintbrush, bitterroot, penstemon, arrow-leaf balsamroot, lupine, and wild onions are all prevalent. Their aromas can be smelt as the blooms race the rising temperatures. Early and late spring depending on rainfall will add beautiful colors to the hillsides.

Reptiles, birds, mammals and larger animals are represented as well. Lizards, squirrels, and the cyclical jackrabbit are all long time desert dwellers. Active during the day, these desert creatures are usually easily seen. Nighttime brings out the more secretive creatures, bats, nighthawks, and rodents, which tend to cause more mischief with unattended camp food and other objects. Pocket mice, deer mice, kangaroo rats all love to gnaw and otherwise turn functional clothes and sleeping bags into hole filled garments! As night falls, the larger mammals also take to the steppes. Skunks, badgers, raccoons, and the ubiquitous coyote, whose moonlight yapping serenades the darkness and those who choose to sleep out under its bright starry skies. The largest animals, pronghorn Antelope, deer, and elk are also inhabitants of this vast and varied country. The signature reptile, the rattlesnake, called by many locals a buzztail is alive and well. Truly a shy creature, they make their abode in this wild and lonely land, camouflaged with an intricate and delicate checkering which blends into their desert home as only nature can. Please remember that these reptiles are not aggressive, and will do all they can to move away from their human intruders. It is NOT in good style to provoke, kill, or otherwise enrage these snakes. Left to their own device, they will retreat from human contact quickly and quietly. Typically only active during the warm part of the day, they are just another cog in the complexity of the desert ecosystem.

The raptors, eagles, hawks and vultures circle high overhead, while small birds, including quail and chukar partridge can be heard near water during the morning dawn and at dusk. The fast disappearing sage grouse dancing around his mating ground, called leks, chest pulsing and expanding as they strut for females is a sight few observe. So involved with their dance, and so often remote, they will take little notice of riders sitting on quiet bikes watching their performance. Watch and remember, as we have no idea how long this species will continue before it fades to a memory and a paragraph in a nature text.

The ghost of the desert, the Mountain Lion is alive and well in Owyhee country, but rarely are they seen in the light of day. Only in the most remote canyons and during brief and rare encounters will you get to witness this graceful and beautiful of cats. The stealth and invisibility of the lion are legendary, and you are fortunate indeed if an opportunity to observe is presented. Finally, the icon of the desert, the majestic Desert Bighorn Sheep who makes his home in the most difficult and inaccessible canyons, climbing, scrambling, and watching for danger. Innately curious, the bighorn will come to strange sounds and sights, to observe, and to see if danger is present. Usually found at the top of the canyon rim looking down, they are forever scanning the distance with their binocular strength eyes. My most memorable experience involving bighorns was during a river trip on a tributary of the Owyhee River. Three ewes swam across the creek not 30 feet in front of my kayak while I floated, open-mouthed towards them. They proceeded to shake themselves off on the bank before walking off and climbing up the canyon side, never once looking back at our small group.

Early man has inhabited the desert country for many centuries. Evidence has shown that as far back as 14-15,000 years people were in the area. Shoshone and Bannock tribes are native to this area. Endowed with the knowledge of the country, and capable of living off what nature provided, they hunted, fished, gathered, and left evidence of their travels all throughout this land. They sought after the meat of the deer, elk and sheep, fished for salmon along the Snake River and its tributaries, and gathered plants such as the beautiful and petite bitterroot and wild onion. Early man was in tune with this country. Pictographs and petroglyphs dot the landscape, and give us vivid and visual reminders of their presence. These signs and shapes are visual clues, but what they truly mean and why are still a source of discussion to this day. Regardless, the rocks that have been carved are a stimulant to discussion and emotions of our generation. Artifacts, arrowheads, smoke stained cave ceilings and campsites dot the landscape, and continue to remind us that for all this lonely and vast land, we are not the first to wander here.

Even the name Owyhee is steeped in history and mystery. Trappers first came to the area with the Donald McKenzie expedition of 1818. Included in the expedition were 3 Hawaiian islanders. These 3 went off exploring, and were never heard from again. The river and the surrounding country became the Owyhee, an improper pronunciation of the word Hawaiian.

The discovery of gold brought settlers to the general Boise Basin area and it was not long before they traveled into the Owyhee area as well. In 1863 gold was discovered along what became Jordan Creek, and the rush was on. A tremendous volume of gold and silver was taken from the mineral rich area. One old story proclaims that Sinker creek was named for so many gold nuggets that they used them for fishing sinkers! Booming mine towns like Ruby City, Flint, Booneville, Fairview, DeLamar, and Silver City became homes to thousands of immigrants. While the gold played out, silver discoveries became more and more valuable. Mines like the Poorman, Orofinio, Morning Star, and War Eagle became rich strikes. Some historians have claimed that the Poorman was one of the greatest veins of silver ever discovered.

With the growth of these mines, food and services were needed as well. Ranchers began running sheep and cattle in from the east and west to feed the growing settlements. These ranches were the beginning of the agricultural foundations of the modern day Treasure Valley. Early ranches such as the Joyce Ranch, established in 1865, and still in use today, the Colette along Castle Creek, the Brace Ranch, and Star Ranch on Juniper Mountain represent the history of the independent rancher. Many other ranches are steeped in multi generational families and provided the goods to support the mining communities. There are many reminders of these hardy souls throughout the area. Cemeteries, mines and homesteads dot the landscape, and give us harsh reminders of what it might have been like living in these places. A sea of sagebrush and other native grasses met the immigrants. Quaking aspens and juniper dotted the hillsides, and their fall colors infused the area with shades of gold. But miners needed wood for their mines, for shoring up the tunnels that began to riddle the mountainsides. The hillsides soon became barren of all vegetation.

Stage routes were needed to transport miners, businessmen, and investors to the area. Toll roads, freight lines and stage stops were built as the population and demand for access grew. Indian uprisings, along with the sheer distance between Boise, Oregon, Nevada and the minefields prompted layover locations and some of these stations and stage houses are still standing to this day. Poison Creek, Wickahoney, Mud Flat, Innskip, and Rockville are still accessible, some in ruin, and others in remarkable condition.

This Owyhee country is a large and varied land. It will always be in a sense desperate. Desperate to live in, desperate to travel through, and oftentimes desperate to understand. But through it all it will always be a proud land, standing tall and prominent in the growth of our nation and its history.

Succor Creek State Park and Succor Creek Canyon.

Chapter 3

Area Descriptions

I have divided the area up into 6 distinctive areas for ease of identification. Specific roads or highways border each area, and they are as follows:

Area 1:

The northern boundary runs from approximately Vale Oregon, west on Oregon State Highway 20 past Harper and to approximately Juntura. Running south from Juntura there is no real defined western boundary, but a general occurring southern line that tends to follow the Harney Malheur county line before finally intersecting Oregon State Hwy 78 on its way to Burns Junction. From here the southern boundary line follows US Hwy 95 to Rome. From Rome the eastern boundary follows the Owyhee Rivers' western side to the Owyhee Reservoir. (Both west and east sides of Owyhee Reservoir are included in this area.) Then uses the Leslie Gulch road as a southern boundary all the way to US Hwy 95. Following this north to Homedale, Idaho, and then on Oregon State Hwy 201 up to its junction with Oregon State Hwy 20 and back to its start in Vale.

Area 2:

At the Leslie Gulch road for the northern edge to US Hwy 95 on the east (McBride Cr.), then south on 95 to Jordan Valley Oregon. US 95 is the southern boundary, and going west on 95 to Rome. From Rome, the line goes up the Owyhee River back to the Leslie Gulch road for the western boundary.

Area 3:

From the Marsing, Idaho bridge, following the Snake River to Grandview, Idaho. This will be the northern and eastern border. Leaving Grandview, the Poison Creek/ Mud Flat road is the southern boundary line heading west all the way to Jordan Valley Oregon. From Jordan Valley the western line will be US Hwy 95 back to Marsing and the bridge.

Area 4:

From Rome Oregon moving south along the West Side of the Owyhee River until the state line. Follow the Idaho Oregon State line to the Nevada border. This is the eastern side of the area. The southern border follows the Nevada Oregon State line to US Hwy 95 at McDermitt Nevada, and then runs north along US Hwy 95 to Burns Junction and on to the start at Rome Oregon.

Area 5:

This area is bordered on the north by US Hwy 95 from Rome Oregon and continues onto the Mud Flat Road finally finishing in Grandview Idaho. From Grandview it runs south along Sate Hwy 78 to its junction with State Hwy 51 just prior to Bruneau, and continues to the Idaho Nevada State line to form the western boundary. The southern boundary follows the Idaho Nevada border to the Oregon border where all three states intersect. From here it goes north and shares the line with Area 4 up along the state line and then up the river and back to Rome.

Area 6:

The western boundary shares the west side of Area 5. At the Northern side, from the junction of Hwy 78 and 51 the line moves to Bruneau Idaho, and follows State Hwy 78 until it crosses the Snake River. From here the line follows the Snake River to the Twin Falls county, Elmore county, and finally Owyhee county line.

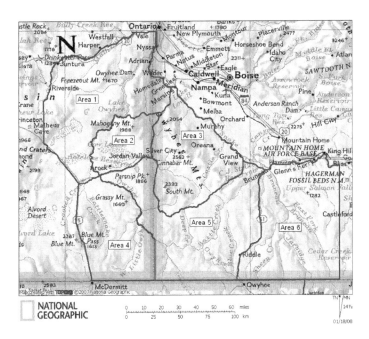

This county line runs south until reaching the Nevada State line. (The Jarbidge Canyon is also included in this area. It is the only gas available so will be necessary for navigation purposes. It is reached by following the Three Creek Road over into Nevada and into the town of Jarbidge.) The line then follows the Idaho Nevada State line back to Idaho State Hwy 51 to the west forming the southern boundary.

Chapter 4

GPS Navigation, Maps, and Mapping Software

The use of A GPS unit along with a map will more than likely be your main method of planning, plotting, and riding a specific route. I am by no means an expert on the makes and models of today's market. The technology industry is booming, and as soon as you pick a unit to use, there will be a new bigger better model to purchase. The use of a GPS is not difficult, nor is it hard to learn the features that are available on any given model. Much like cell phones, they typically have more features than necessary, and many are never used. Suffice to say that whatever model you choose, you need to bone up and become an expert on the specific functions that are important or pertinent to your use. I have used throughout this guidebook process an older model Garmin E-Trex GPS unit. This was an originally inexpensive and very simple unit. I use it mainly for keeping tracks, that is my actual path I have ridden on any given trip. It has limitations, but I have learned what they are and adjust accordingly. I use it for basic waypoint marking, as well as for general waypoint route finding. I rarely use it for true routes. It has many limitations, but conversely it also provides me with a limited number of choices with which to make a mistake on as well.

On any given ride I use my GPS for tracking my route or path, and then save this information to my mapping software (computer). I also pre-load waypoints with which to follow routes (drawn from the same mapping software) in a more precise manner, and for setting waypoints where crucial directional information is necessary. Sometimes I will even mark a waypoint with a specific directional note such as "RIGHT" or "LEFT". This is just what I have been used to, and really is just personal preference and habit. It doesn't have the capability of the newer and more modern units. New and "smarter" GPS units are now equipped with pre-loaded information, road systems, restaurants, and even gas locations. With the advent of the tiny SD cards, huge amounts of information are at our fingertips. The ability to download entire maps, complete with your intended routes and regions will be a huge advantage over the old systems.

I have my small Garmin mounted to my handlebars with a RAM mounting system. It is a small but simple system that I have raced with, crashed with, and generally abused without any problems. You can spend as much or as little as you choose on a myriad of GPS units and their respective mounting equipment. The choice is yours. It seems that the general consensus with regard to brand has been either Garmin or Magellan brands. Models range from simple to approaching Star Trek capabilities.

In conjunction with the GPS unit, some form of maps and mapping ability will be critical for route finding and location information. This being either the physical maps of varying degrees of scale, or computer generated software-mapping functions that interface with your GPS, or a combination of the two. These software programs are now readily available, and are quite remarkable. I have found that by combining the two you can achieve a very high degree of information with a relatively simple approach. Mapping paper such as National Geographic adventure paper allows the custom printing of maps detailed for your chosen routes. I have been using the National Geographic TOPO series of software, and have had great results and solid reliability. All of the routes and trips in this guidebook were used with this software.

Whatever your GPS, maps, or mapping software choices are, become intimately familiar with all of their functions. As in so many applications, the little "tricks" are what usually save the day. One example is the ability to zoom in and zoom out to make sure that closely situated roads don't confuse you and lead you down a path that ultimately will have to be re-crossed.

Be aware of the limitations of your GPS as well. Deep rocky canyons will block signals and cause a loss of data or signal. The battery demon will eat your juice when you least can afford to lose it. Always bring spare batteries. Cables and mounts will loosen or break. Make sure you have hard copies of your route, cheat sheets, or other written information that can take over if for some reason you cannot get it electronically. Good old fashion road signs with arrows and mileage are always welcome! As you ride, save your route often, mark waypoints at areas or points of interest that you can research or return to at a later date. Stay in tune with your system and use it. Work over your system and all its points to ensure that you will be prepared for most of the epic situations that you are planning on exposing yourself to. Those that you can't prepare for, well, that's why they become epics.

All of the coordinates used in the guidebook are based upon the standard NAD83/WGS84 data, and are listed in Degrees, Minutes, and Seconds. The data can be listed as UTM within specific software applications. I have chosen to use this format because it is what I am comfortable and used to.

Chapter 5

Desert Riding

With over 6 ½ million, that's right 6 ½ MILLION acres to explore, this land we call the Owyhee is huge. Over 2 million acres comprise the rivers and canyon complexes of the Owyhee, Bruneau, and Jarbidge alone. This is truly big country. As Sal Fish said about the land that makes up the longest point to point desert off road race in the world, the Baja 1000, "…it's not for wussies!" The same can be said for the Owyhee and all its vastness.

Local riding areas lend a sense of security, of safety. There are out houses, loading platforms, and pretty map and announcement boards that breed stability and predictability. The true Owyhee desert holds no such illusions, no such stability, and no such predictability. There is nothing that can prepare you for the sheer size of this land. It has been said that there is no location outside of Alaska, no place in the lower 48 states that is farther from a piece of pavement than here. It is very possible to run through an entire tank of gas, fill up from an emergency bottle, and still never come close to a gas station. This area is not for the faint of heart. It will spank you and leave you in tears in an instant and with no regrets. You must change your mindset and your habits here if you hope to be successful, read survive. The desert will dictate all, and we can do nothing but smile and adapt within its ever-changing landscape.

I remember a nice evening ride up to Spanish Charley. It was warm and calm; we were dressed in typical summer riding pants and jerseys. We watched the lightning flashes to the west and were amazed at the colors of the sky. Minutes later the sky exploded around us and the rain and hail came down. We rode crazily for a rock outcropping, slipping and sliding on the instantly muddy trail, abandoned our bikes, and ran for cover, squeezing together under what shelter we could find. We emerged 20 minutes later, cold, shivering, soaked, and acutely aware that we would be negotiating many rough spots in the dark before we made it back to the car that night.

Fall and spring rides are just one tick away from an early or late season snow storm that will have you camped under a juniper for the next 24 hours with no way to alert anyone that you will probably be late for work on Monday. There will be no one to call, no one to pick up you, or your bike.

A rider must be entirely self-sufficient, totally self-supported and willing to deal with the setbacks that are sure to come. This is adventure riding in the simplest, the truest form. Flat tires, mechanical difficulties, or becoming lost are simple items at the local trailhead. They are small issues with the car just over the hill in the parking lot. However, 120 miles from the nearest asphalt is not the time to learn how to change a flat tire with your new trail tire irons that you have never used before. Would you like to find out that the Phillips screwdriver you have as an attachment to your fancy tool won't reach your carburetor bowl screws 90 miles out when your gas begins to leak? You must learn to think outside the box. The rules are not written, and those that are, well, they usually aren't followed. The responsibility lies with you, the rider, and no one else. YOU MUST NEVER FORGET THIS! Granted, you will be found, but how many days later and in what condition is anyone's guess. I can't say it any plainer; people die out here!

Complete and functional tool kits, tire repair kits, and a McGyver type of mindset will be your only support for these rides. Your imagination will be stretched, your mechanical skills tested, your patience emptied,

A McGyver mindset and the ability to work on your bike are essential. On the road to Silver City, the Queen of Idaho's Ghost Towns.

and still it might not be enough. Coupled with on the spot road building, bridge engineering and construction, and fence repair you will have a few tall tales to tell around the winter fire. The Owyhee brings its own style of luck, and maybe it will smile on you.

You never know, you might even convince a friend to ride with you next season.

Chapter 6

Equipment

It's not my intent or place to use this guide to dictate bike requirements, or equipment details. Its been documented regularly about the man who went around the world on a Honda trail 90 with a bedroll on his handlebars. My desire is to simply impress upon all who choose to ride in this area to be AWARE of what they are getting in to. The rider who chooses to ride from Boise to the Owyhee River Canyonlands and back on a 125cc bike with a stock gas tank and knobby tires might look a bit more closely at the implications that choice might present. Sure you can do it, but do you want too? Modern day dual sport bikes, typically in the 350cc to 1200cc ranges are well documented and present many options for traveling safely and comfortably. Do your own research. Decide upon your use and desire and then go pester your motorcycle dealer and salespersons for even more information. Ask local clubs, go online and join forums, peruse magazines and make an informed decision on what size and color your ultimate machine will be.

But remember there is a joker in this deck. The desert and its long-range travels dictate to a great degree our bike set-ups and expectations. We must be alert to what we will encounter on these tours, these excursions we call rides. First and foremost is the fuel issue. Larger, "desert" tanks are a necessity to make it from gas to gas. Many times we are required to travel long distances between fuel. Some times we have to bring it, in the form of extra tanks or bottles. Other times we can roll into a small mom and pop service station on reserve and just smile.

Mechanically sound and dependable machines are necessary for the wear and tear that will be heaped upon our bikes. Bringing spare and necessary parts is another item to observe. From the smallest nuts and bolts to extra plugs and levers, all are important. The infamous zip ties and duct tape are all well documented "save the day" items. Well maintained wheels, tires, chains and sprockets are critical items. Being able to service them in any place and at any time is an essential skill. After all, the whole idea of two wheels is based upon the principle of rolling down the road. Breaking down 65 miles from your last gas stop due to not carrying a spare master link is truly an amateur move. Hand guards, flexible levers, skid plates, case guards, radiator guards are all after market products that make sense. Research will show which bikes are in need of what types of modifications to make them even more trustworthy and reliable.

Each route should be considered carefully before undertaking. A GPS, their mounts and other technical items are available from many manufacturers. There are entire luggage systems now available, with some even allowing for additional fuel or water carrying capacities. Take advantage of these items. Give yourself some peace of mind by using equipment and modifications that stack the odds in your favor.

We have the ability to enjoy many levels of adventure without putting ourselves in harms way. Always alert someone as to your intended route of travel and when you will be back. Simple common sense in the desert is usually the difference between walking and having a great adventure that you can share with the guys during the winter BS sessions.

Being mentally, physically and mechanically prepared is the responsibility of the rider. The consequences of not being prepared are usually immediate, intense, and often painful. Breaking down, over heating, or becoming injured is not a pleasant option. Prepare correctly, and enjoy the journey.

Always respect the trails and roads; treat them with their just do. Stay on them, and understand our impact with regards to erosion, noise, dust, litter, and fire. Obey all regulations put forth by the local jurisdictions for your trips. It is your responsibility to understand and be in compliance with the local regulations. Many watch our use of the land and we need to be on our best behavior at all times.

As a last note, there are many clubs and organizations that continue to do a tremendous amount of behind the scene work to keep our lands open and available to us as riders. Through many hours of conversation and volunteer work, they have developed priceless relationships with the Agencies who direct and implement the rules and regulations that we are held to. Support them, learn from them and become an advocate for better and more multi user land use.

Chapter 7

Routes and Route Finding Skills

Route finding skills in the desert are not easily learned. In general it can be a bewildering experience. Large open vistas stretch for many miles. Landmarks with no recognizable features are few and far between. Few signs, and a feeling of remoteness can lead to worried looks and finally apprehension as you pass faint cross roads and trails leading off into the distance.

Poor information and vague descriptions have led many desert travelers to never arrive at their intended destination. I cannot express enough the reliance on good route finding skills, patience, and an open-minded attitude. A "seeing where this road might lead too" are pre-requisites of the Owyhee traveler. Yes you will turn around many times, but you will also discover hidden gems, see wildlife, and ultimately discover that the road did indeed go where you hoped.

GPS, Topo maps, and local surface maps are all great references, but I have had all of them not work at one time or another, leaving me to wonder just where in the hell I am!

Technically speaking, route finding skills are derived from two areas. The first would be the use of a GPS, maps and other written or acquired information that helps to dictate where you are headed for. Using GPS generated software routes, printed and marked up maps, and information from locals would be examples.

Second would be the physical ability to put your iron steed through a large and varied landscape. This could be anything from tire shredding rocks to engine overheating deep sand. The all time famous, or infamous Owyhee Gumbo falls into a class of its own. A mud formed from rains or other moisture, it turns the first 1-4" of surface material into something of a cross between slick and slicker then goose you know what. The hard pack underneath this mud will allow no traction worth mentioning, and so begins the game of keeping not only the rear of the bike behind you, but a grim struggle to just stay upright. You will never forget your first battle with the gumbo.

Mechanically speaking, it bears repeating. You are ON YOUR OWN! There are no AAA trucks to come bail you out. Pure backcountry ingenuity is your only friend. Duct tape, zip ties and baling wire has seen many a trip finished with stories to tell. Electronic devices, such as a GPS and the connections will break, needing back up methods to keep them in working condition. Any and everything that can possibly break or cease to function will. Murphy has a second home here in the Owyhee country. Maybe that's why the county seat is named for him.

The routes that are described in this guidebook are based upon a few specific lines of reference. I felt that it was important to put the routes into some form of descriptive jargon that would allow a grading system to be used. Route descriptions, difficulties, and the length of trips are set up using a scale similar to the one used for guidebooks on hiking and climbing. First will be a Roman numeral grade that denotes the overall time commitment. The second rating will be the degree of technical difficulty, which I have divided into three levels, easy, moderate, and difficult. These levels will dictate the degree of skill needed to physically pilot your bike through the route. Also included will be a general trip length in miles, a starting and stopping point complete with GPS coordinates. The generally accepted local or map used names for mountains, streams, creeks, landmarks, towns and roads. Any important directional information will be included along with the respective GPS coordinates. I have no intentions of providing a follow the numbers travel guide. I only hope to give you the basic information as to allow you to pursue your own exploration and adventure.

Roman Numeral Scale:

I   Short trip, lasting less than half a day.

II   Longer trips lasting most of the day.

III   Trips needing the entire day.

IV   Trips needing the entire day, returning during darkness, or very possibly spending the night.

V   Adventure touring with planned overnight expectations.

Be advised that your skills and your routes can have a dramatic effect on what the time and degree of difficulty you will encounter. These are subjective ratings at best. Some riders might consider a 70-mile ride to be short, where others feel that is a long day. Typical overnight rides or long weekend rides will range from 200 to 500 mile lengths depending on difficulty.

Technical difficulties:

Easy   Gravel roads passable for high clearance vehicles but not necessarily 4wd. The Mud Flat Road, Leslie Gulch Road, or Jordan Craters Road would be examples.

Moderate   Rough double tracks and other rocky or 4wd type of roads where rocks, ruts and other obstacles are to be encountered. Examples would be the Owyhee Ridge, Owyhee Ridge Horse Trap, and Owyhee Reservoir Dam areas.

Difficult   These are faint double tracks and severely challenging terrain that might include sandy washes, rocks, steep inclines, wash outs, water crossings, limited signage and fuel access. These forays will also entail route finding and directional challenges. Examples would be the Battle Creek track, Lambert Table, and Bull Basin rides.

Directional Arrows

I have used directional arrows to further denote specific turn by turn directions. These arrows are to provide more detail at crucial intersections. The arrows are used as follows:

→ Right Turn, Stay Right, Bear right, or generally ignore any other turn that could lead you otherwise.

← Left Turn, Stay Left, Bear left, or generally ignore any other turn that could lead you otherwise.

↑ Stay Forward, not necessarily straight. I use this sparingly, as many intersections are not a typical straight line. Usually used in conjunction with a four-way decision, or when traveling forward is a more obvious choice. I wanted to stay away from this sign, and have used left and right arrows more often.

Negotiating Owyhee gumbo from a brief
thunderstorm on Juniper Mountian

Chapter 8

Routes

Area 1 Route 1 - Succor Creek Canyon

Topo 7.5" series: Adrian, OR ID
Graveyard Point, ID OR, Owyhee Ridge, OR, Three
  Fingers Rock, OR, Pole Creek Top, OR ID, Rock-
  ville, OR ID, Sheaville, OR ID
Grade II
Difficulty: Easy
Route Start: Approximately 7 miles from Homedale Id.
  Bridge. Idaho Hwy 19, Oregon Hwy 201
Length of route: 35 miles to OR Hwy 95 (Leslie Gulch
  Rd.)
Starting coords: 43°37'48" N, 117°03'38" W
Finish coords: 43°13'38" N, 117°03'15" W

Route description:

← 43°37'48" N, 117°03'38" W
Follow south on well-maintained gravel road.
→ 43°33'28" N, 117°06'37" W access to Camp Kettle
  Cr., Three Fingers Rock & Owyhee Reservoir
← 43°27'13" N, 117°07'13" W
Succor Cr. Bridge. Eastern access to Jump Cr. areas.
← 43°25'51" N, 117°07'08" W
Succor Cr. ford.
→ 43°23'36" N, 117°07'45" W

Western access to Negro Rock, Horse Trap Spring,
  McIntyre Ridge
→ 43°19'15" N, 117°06'56" W
Western access to Steamboat Ridge, Leslie Gulch
← 43°19'03" N, 117°06'55" W
→ 43°19'03" N, 117°06'32" W
Rockville School
→ 43°14'45" N, 117°05'49" W Mahogany Gap access
43°13'38" N, 117°03'15" W Hwy 95

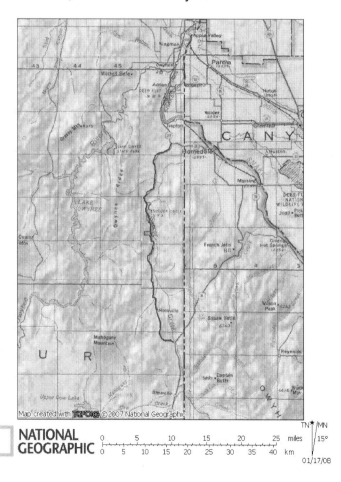

Map created with TOPO!© 2007 National Geographic

**NATIONAL
GEOGRAPHIC**

| 0 | 5 | 10 | 15 | 20 | 25 | miles |
| 0 | 5 | 10 | 15 | 20 | 25 | 30 | 35 | 40 | km |

TN↑ /MN
15°
01/17/08

Mainly good gravel roads, Succor Creek Canyon boasts some of the most colorful and stunning spires, cliff faces and jagged rocks in the area. Fossil beds, opals, and thunder eggs are native to the area. The road is also a main access point to many side trails. A state park with camping and outhouse facilities is also available at the bridge. (Note, the bridge is closed to full size vehicles, but bikes are still able to cross it) After leaving the Rockville area, the road winds back east to Hwy 95 and the asphalt.

Area 1 Route 2 – Three Finger Rocks

Topo 7.5" series: Adrian, OR ID
Graveyard Point, ID OR
Owyhee Ridge, OR
Three Fingers Rock, OR
Bannock Ridge, OR
Grade II
Difficulty: Moderate due to very rocky roads, washed
    out areas and remoteness.
Route Start: Approximately 7 miles from Homedale Id.
    Bridge. Idaho Hwy 19, Oregon Hwy 201
Length of route: 28 miles to Leslie Gulch Rd. connec-
    tion.
Starting coords: 43°37'48" N, 117°03'38" W
Finish coords: 43°20'17" N, 117°06'48" W

Route description:

← 43°37'48" N, 117°03'38" W
→ 43°33'28" N, 117°06'36" W
← 43°32'10" N, 117°11'00" W
← 43°31'34" N, 117°10'52" W

← 43°30'10" N, 117°11'21" W
← 43°29'38" N, 117°11'17" W
← 43°29'20" N, 117°11'16" W

* → Painted Canyon & Carlton Canyon Access

→ 43°26'41" N, 117°09'53" W
→ 43°26'04" N, 117°09'27" W

* ← Horse Trap Spring

43°23'13" N, 117°09'10" W Saddle Butte Reservoir
← 43°22'57" N, 117°11'12" W
← 43°20'19" N, 117°10'46" W
← 43°20'16" N, 117°10'24" W
← 43°20'10" N, 117°08'15" W
43°20'17" N, 117°06'48" W Succor Creek Road

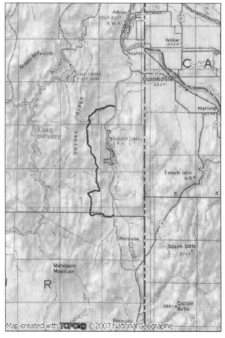

NATIONAL
GEOGRAPHIC

0   5   10   15   20   25 miles
0   5   10   15   20   25   30   35   40 km

TN MN
15°
01/16/08

Access to Painted Canyon, Carlton Canyon and the Honeycombs. Slot canyons and incredible geology.

Three Fingers Rock, a huge basalt outcropping shaped as its name implies. Steep walls and fabulous views. The route basically parallels Succor Creek Canyon, and there are additional East/West alternative routes to gain the canyon access. This area was well known for its colorful buckaroo cowboys.

Area 1   Route 3 – Owyhee Ridge Horse Trap

Topo 7.5" series: Adrian, OR ID
Graveyard Point, ID OR, Owyhee Ridge, OR, Three
  Fingers Rock, OR, Bannock Ridge, OR
Grade III
Difficulty: Moderate due to rocky roads, washed out
  areas, some technical riding and remoteness.
Route Start: Approximately 7 miles from Homedale Id.
  Bridge. Idaho Hwy 19, Oregon Hwy 201
Length of route: 27 miles to horse trap, an additional 8
  miles back to Leslie Gulch Rd. and 11 miles back to
  Succor Cr. Canyon Rd.
Starting coords: 43°35'48" N, 117°06'44" W
Finish coords: 43°23'26" N, 117°16'52" W

Route description:

← 43°37'48" N, 117°03'38" W Succor Cr. Rd.
→ 43°35'48" N, 117°06'43" W
→ 43°35'49" N, 117°10'18" W
← 43°36'06" N, 117°12'01" W
↑ 43°35'13" N, 117°12'36" W
← 43°34'56" N, 117°13'06" W

← 43°33'32" N, 117°13'11" W
← 43°30'56" N, 117°13'59" W
→ 43°30'10" N, 117°13'11" W
→ 43°28'54" N, 117°13'44" W
← 43°28'33" N, 117°14'10" W
* → Painted Canyon access
→ 43°28'11" N, 117°14'07" W
→ 43°24'36" N, 117°14'18" W
* ← Three Finger Gulch access
→ 43°22'27" N, 117°14'03" W
* ← Succor Cr. Rd. access
→ 43°22'25" N, 117°15'35" W
43°23'26" N, 117°16'52" W Horse Trap

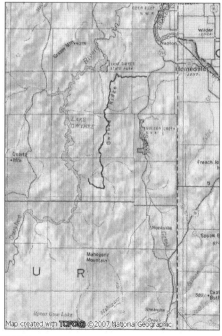

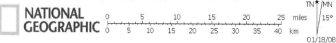

Map created with TOPO!© ©2007 National Geographic

NATIONAL
GEOGRAPHIC

| 0 | 5 | 10 | 15 | 20 | 25 miles |
| 0 | 5 | 10 | 15 | 20 | 25 | 30 | 35 | 40 km |

TN ⚹ /MN
/15°
01/18/08

You might have GPS difficulty in some of the deeper canyons. A few side trails are difficult to spot. Good route finding skills are needed for this ride. This horse trap is reported to be over one hundred years old, and was constructed in a natural bottleneck of the canyon. Indians and cowboys alike have used it and there are stories of up to 1500 wild horses being trapped here over the years. This area is loaded with wild game and upland birds. Be careful of buzz tails as the weather heats up. Don't miss the downstream cave. It might be possible to walk (ride?) this creek bottom all the way to the reservoir at certain times of the year.

Area 1 Route 4 – Owyhee Reservoir Dam

Topo 7.5" series: Adrian, OR ID
Owyhee Ridge, OR
Owyhee Dam, OR
Grade I
Difficulty: Moderate due to rocky roads, seldom used
  trail.
Route Start: Approximately 7 miles from Homedale Id.
  Bridge. Idaho Hwy 19, Oregon Hwy 201
Length of route: 30-mile loop from Succor Cr. Canyon
  road.
Starting coords: 43°35'48" N, 117°06'44" W
Finish coords: 43°36'04" N, 117°12'02" W

Route description:

← 43°37'48" N, 117°03'38" W. Succor Cr. Rd.
→ 43°35'48" N, 117°06'44" W
→ 43°36'04" N, 117°12'02" W
← 43°37'19" N, 117°11'35" W

← 43°37'52" N, 117°13'03" W
← 43°39'10" N, 117°14'01" W
← 43°39'22" N, 117°15'25" W Asphalt road to Owyhee
  State Park
← 43°36'23" N, 117°15'16" W
← 43°34'57" N, 117°13'06" W
→ 43°36'04" N, 117°12'02" W
End of loop

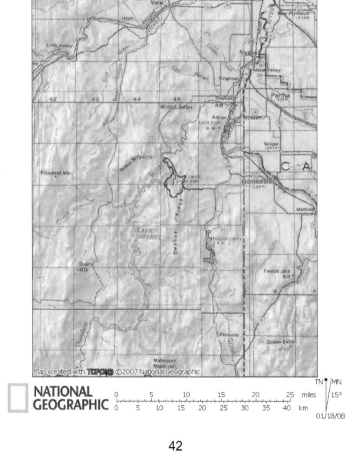

NATIONAL
GEOGRAPHIC

0   5   10   15   20   25 miles

0 5 10 15 20 25 30 35 40 km

TN ↑ /MN
  15°

01/18/08

Seldom-used roads lead to Owyhee Reservoir. The route comes in from above the dam, and leaves from the resort area to climb back up the canyon walls and over to Succor Cr. Canyon Rd. Beautiful views and close proximity make it a good local albeit rough ride when time is short.

At the time of its construction, Owyhee Dam was the tallest dam in the world at 417 feet high. Construction began in 1928, and was finished in 1932. The Glory Hole drain is visible and is a 309-foot vertical shaft that drains to a 700-foot tunnel through the dam.

Area 1 Route 5 – Spanish Charlie Gravesite

Topo 7.5" series:
Jump Creek Canyon, ID, Pole Creek Top, OR ID
Grade I
Difficulty: Moderate, with difficult washed out and steep climbing.
Route Start: Jump Creek 43°30'07" N, 116°54'36" W
Length of route: 35 mile loop
Starting coords: 43°30'07" N, 116°54'36" W
Finish coords: 43°26'14" N, 117°06'01" W

Route description:

43°30'07" N, 116°54'36" W
43°30'10" N, 116°56'15" W Poison Creek Stage Station
← 43°29'49" N, 116°57'26" W
→ 43°29'03" N, 116°58'31" W
← 43°29'28" N, 116°59'03" W start of steep technical descent

43°29'38" N, 117°00'02" W Strodes Basin/Pond
43°29'36" N, 117°00'19" W
← 43°29'52" N, 117°00'39" W
← 43°30'03" N, 117°03'18" W
← 43°27'34" N, 117°06'51" W
← 43°26'24" N, 117°06'36" W
43°26'14" N, 117°05'59" W Gravesite

Extremely obscure ride to a very mysterious and interesting gravesite. Spanish Charley built a small dugout,

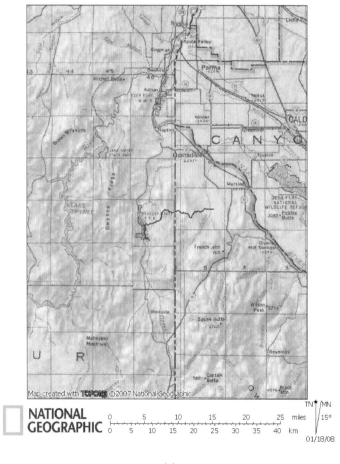

barn and corrals complete with a rock fence encircling his small ranch with the double pitchfork brand. Rumor has it that a local rancher had sheep on the place, and Spanish went to look. Some form of altercation took place and he was shot and killed by James Mussel. Mussel was tried and acquitted of the crime, and lost his sheep for the cost of defense and trial. Mussel went on to settle in the area, built the Homedale Ferry, and actually submitted the name for the town (Homedale) in 1900. The enormous rock fence that was built by hard labor to the north and east is still quite visible. As you crest the steep hill be aware of the intense geological colors at work in the soil to the west.

Area 2 Route 6 – Leslie Gulch

Topo 7.5" series: Piute Butte, ID, Rockville, OR ID,
  Bannock Ridge, OR, Rooster Comb, OR
Grade II
Difficulty: Easy gravel roads
Route Start: Hwy 95, 22 miles from Marsing, ID
  bridge.
Length of route: 25 miles to Leslie Gulch.
Starting coords: 43°18'34" N, 116°58'54" W
Alternate Start: 43°13'38" N, 117°03'15" W
Finish coords: 43°19'20" N, 117°19'24" W

Route description:

→ 43°18'34" N, 116°58'54" W
← 43°20'06" N, 117°01'52" W
→ 43°19'59" N, 117°02'36" W
43°19'37" N, 117°03'55" W Rockville Cemetery
← 43°19'57" N, 117°04'48" W

→ 43°19'03" N, 117°06'32" W Rockville School site
→ 43°19'03" N, 117°06'56" W
← 43°19'15" N, 117°06'56" W
← 43°20'10" N, 117°08'13" W
43°19'20" N, 117°19'24" W Owyhee Reservoir

Alt Start:

→ 43°13'38" N, 117°03'15" W
→ 43°14'45" N, 117°05'49" W
43°17'32" N, 117°06'15" W Rockville Site
43°19'03" N, 117°06'32" W join route here

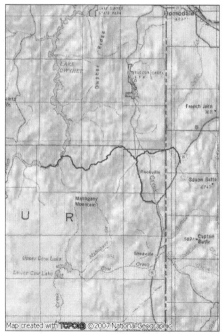

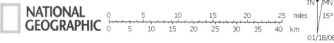

The alternate start is farther down US HWY 95, and follows Succor Cr. up to the Rockville School junction. You can loop out and cover both sections easily.

Rocks Stage Station site 43°20'33" N, 117°00'06" W is just off the first waypoint turn. Unbelievable canyon carved by wind, rain, and erosion. Tremendous rock faces of many colors and shapes. Steep climb into and out of the canyon that ends at access to Owyhee Reservoir. Bighorn Sheep inhabit the area and numerous hiking trails abound. Do not attempt the grade in wet conditions! For the truly adventuresome, there is a hot spring that is accessible in low water conditions along the shoreline about 4 miles upstream from the boat ramp. This canyon is not to be missed!

The spectacular canyon of Leslie Gulch

Area 2 Route 7 – Mahogany Mountain

Topo 7.5" series: Sheaville, OR ID, Mahogany Gap,
  OR, McCain Creek, OR, Downey Canyon, OR
Grade III
Difficulty: Moderate
Route Start: 3 miles from Hwy 95, 43°13'37" N,
  117°03'15" W
Length of route: 35 mile loop.
Starting coords: 43°14'45" N, 117°05'50" W
Finish coords: 43°12'52" N, 117°09'42" W

Route description:

← 43°14'45" N, 117°05'50" W
→ 43°11'59" N, 117°10'49" W
→ 43°12'36" N, 117°11'10" W
→ 43°12'59" N, 117°12'00" W
← 43°13'56" N, 117°12'18" W
→ 43°14'46" N, 117°13'34" W
→ 43°14'55" N, 117°14'37" W
→ 43°14'32" N, 117°15'08" W Fish Cr. access
← 43°13'43" N, 117°15'52" W
* → Gunsight Pass 43°13'46" N, 117°16'05" W
← 43°09'36" N, 117°15'35" W
← 43°07'24" N, 117°14'31" W
← 43°07'08" N, 117°13'43" W
← 43°08'01" N, 117°12'37" W
→ 43°08'34" N, 117°12'27" W
* ← Fish Cr. access
→ 43°08'52" N, 117°11'38" W
← 43°08'52" N, 117°11'01" W
← 43°09'32" N, 117°10'52" W
→ 43°12'05" N, 117°10'47" W
43°11'59" N, 117°10'49" W re-joins starting point

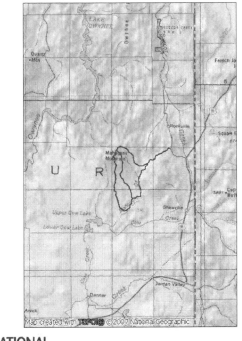

TN ★ /MN

| 0 | 5 | 10 | 15 | 20 | 25 | miles | 15° |

| 0 | 5 | 10 | 15 | 20 | 25 | 30 | 35 | 40 | km |

01/18/08

This ride circumnavigates Mahogany Mountain by climbing the north side, to a point just short of Gunsight Pass, and then drops down the southern side and follows Mahogany Creek back and through Mahogany Gap, then back to the start of the loop. To reach Gunsight Pass, continue on only ¼ mile farther. There is also a trail up Fish Creek 43°08'36" N, 117°12'27" W. This will take you to the top near Gunsight Pass as well. This is a more technical ride. Tremendous views of the Treasure Valley to the east, and to the west are the Tongue, Blue Canyon, and the Owyhee Breaks.

Area 2 Route 8 – The Owyhee Breaks

Topo 7.5" series: Sheaville, OR ID, Mahogany Gap,
  OR, McCain Creek, OR, Downey Canyon, OR
Grade III
Difficulty: Moderate
Route Start: 3 miles from Hwy 95, 43°13'37" N,
  117°03'15" W
Length of route: 70 mile loop.
Starting coords: 43°14'45" N, 117°05'50" W
Finish coords: 43°18'57" N, 117°28'06" W

Route description:

→ 43°13'37" N, 117°03'15" W
← 43°14'45" N, 117°05'50" W
→ 43°11'59" N, 117°10'49" W
→ 43°14'46" N, 117°13'34" W
→ 43°14'55" N, 117°14'37" W
→ 43°14'32" N, 117°15'08" W
→ 43°13'44" N, 117°15'58" W
← 43°13'47" N, 117°17'09" W
→ 43°12'31" N, 117°19'51" W
→ 43°12'30" N, 117°20'01" W
← 43°14'05" N, 117°21'24" W
→ 43°14'19" N, 117°23'48" W
← 43°15'02" N, 117°23'31" W
* ← The Tongue access
← 43°15'14" N, 117°23'39" W
43°18'57" N, 117°28'06" W Blue Canyon and Owyhee
  River/Reservoir confluence

Large views, wide-open expanses, and few visitors.
You can expect to have this area to yourself if you

choose to go. Here is another rough area of the desert worth visiting.

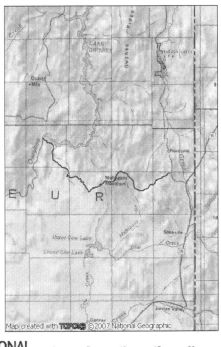

Deep into Owyhee country, the Owyhee Breaks, Blue Canyon, and the Tongue are extremely remote. They offer access to seldom used and seldom seen views of the Owyhee Reservoir and the adjacent canyons. There are multitudes of off shoot tracks that wind throughout this area. The terrain can be very unforgiving. It is possible for this area to be linked north to Leslie Gulch, and farther south to Jordan Craters and Birch Creek. Route finding will be challenging.

Area 2 Route 9 – Coffeepot Crater

Topo 7.5" series: Hooker Creek, OR ID, Downey Canyon, OR, McCain Creek, OR, Jordan Craters North, OR
Grade III
Difficulty: Moderate
Route Start: Hwy 95, 43°05'16" N, 117°03'51" W
Length of route: 26 mile one way.
Starting coords: 43°05'16" N, 117°03'52" W
Finish coords: 43°08'46" N, 117°27'36" W

Route description:

→ 43°05'16" N, 117°03'51" W
→ 43°05'38" N, 117°09'22" W
→ 43°05'04" N, 117°10'41" W
→ 43°05'25" N, 117°12'43" W
→ 43°05'49" N, 117°13'24" W
→ 43°07'24" N, 117°14'36" W
← 43°08'43" N, 117°16'24" W
← 43°09'25" N, 117°18'39" W
← 43°09'31" N, 117°20'44" W
← 43°10'02" N, 117°25'29" W
* → Blowout Reservoir access
← 43°10'04" N, 117°26'56" W
* → Birch Creek access road
← 43°09'27" N, 117°28'17" W
43°08'46" N, 117°27'36" W Coffeepot Crater

Fabulous lava flows, cinder cones, and vent tubes are all within easy reach. A very accessible road into the Jordan Craters lava field. The road can be quite nasty in wet weather. Access to Cow Lakes and the Owyhee River are also available. Online aerial views are truly unbelievable, and are a great research item prior to traveling into the area.

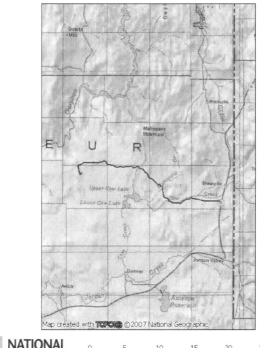

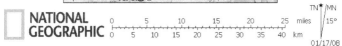

Coffeepot Crater is situated inside the Jordan Craters area. A surreal landscape covered in lava, it is one of the most inhospitable areas in the entire desert. The crater and surrounding lava fields are easily explored. This section of Oregon should not be missed. There is a hiking trail that will lead you down into the extinct crater of the volcano. The flow covers over 29 square miles and has incredibly well preserved flow and vent examples. The volcanic field is part of an almost 155 square mile flow from ages past.

Area 2 Route 10 – Birch Creek, Owyhee River

Topo 7.5" series: Hooker Creek, OR ID, Downey Can-
 yon, OR, McCain Creek, OR, Jordan Craters North,
 OR, The Hole in the Ground, OR
Grade III
Difficulty: Moderate
Route Start: Hwy 95, 43°05'16" N, 117°03'52" W
Length of route: 29 mile one way.
Starting coords: 43°05'16" N, 117°03'52" W
Finish coords: 43°12'54" N, 117°30'11" W

Route description:

→ 43°05'16" N, 117°03'51" W
→ 43°05'38" N, 117°09'22" W
→ 43°05'04" N, 117°10'41" W
→ 43°05'25" N, 117°12'43" W
→ 43°05'49" N, 117°13'24" W
→ 43°07'24" N, 117°14'36" W
← 43°08'43" N, 117°16'24" W
← 43°09'25" N, 117°18'39" W
← 43°09'31" N, 117°20'44" W
← 43°10'02" N, 117°25'29" W
* → Blowout Reservoir access
→ 43°10'04" N, 117°26'56" W
43°12'54" N, 117°30'11" W
 Birch Creek and Owyhee River

Birch Creek is an access for river runners doing the
Owyhee. At the river you can explore both upstream
and down. Low water conditions provide a ford and this
would make for one wild adventure ride if you crossed
over the river and on to Rome, or back to Vale. Trails
lead out to The Hole in the Ground, Greeley Bar, Deer

Park, and the Owyhee Breaks. By turning at Blowout Reservoir you can search for the rock corral used to trap horses in past days. Big country and a beautiful river setting. Say hello to the caretaker. He is a great source of information and news of the area.

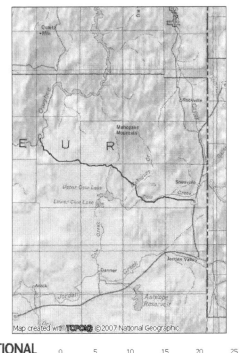

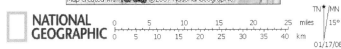

This is the start of an area that could easily be linked to form a myriad of long and overnight tours. Only your fuel range will be a limiting factor. Jordan Valley is situated in a central location and touring this area and to the south and or west is a wide open adventure waiting to happen.

Area 2 Route 11 – Bogus Bench

Topo 7.5" series:

Jordan Craters North, OR, The Hole in the Ground, OR, Rinehart Canyon, OR, Lambert Rocks, OR, Bogus Bench, OR, Arock, OR. Jordan Craters South, OR

Grade IV

Difficulty: Difficult due to distance (100+ mi.), route finding, and terrain.

Route Start: Hwy 95, 43°05'16" N, 117°03'52" W

Length of route: 51 miles from Coffeepot Crater. (See Route 9)

Starting coords: 43°09'28" N, 117°28'17" W

Finish coords: Same.

Route description:

→ 43°09'28" N, 117°28'17" W

→ 43°09'11" N, 117°28'37" W

→ 43°08'42" N, 117°29'25" W

→ 43°08'51" N, 117°30'19" W

→ 43°09'47" N, 117°31'12" W

← 43°10'27" N, 117°32'07" W

→ 43°10'04" N, 117°34'54" W

← 43°09'42" N, 117°35'51" W

→ 43°08'05" N, 117°38'57" W

→ 43°04'09" N, 117°35'47" W

→ **43°02'59" N, 117°36'12" W * Note: Bail out here, Turn LEFT.**

← 43°03'06" N, 117°37'49" W

* → Bogus Ranch 43°03'48" N, 117°39'03" W

← 43°02'24" N, 117°38'29" W

← 43°01'18" N, 117°38'35" W

← 43°00'34" N, 117°38'29" W

← 43°00'07" N, 117°34'18" W
← 42°59'30" N, 117°31'35" W
← 43°00'26" N, 117°31'31" W
← 43°02'35" N, 117°31'22" W
→ **43°03'23" N, 117°32'11" W* Note: connects from Bail out coordinates.**
↑ 43°04'27" N, 117°30'51" W (4 way, stay ↑)
← 43°05'24" N, 117°29'15" W
→ 43°09'11" N, 117°28'37" W

Lava sinks reservoir at 43°01'02" N, 117°35'42" W, Bogus creek lava fields and falls 43°02'59" N, 117°36'12" W.

This route starts after you have reached the last turn for Coffeepot Crater (Route # 9). From there you will travel in a large counterclockwise direction through the Bogus Bench and Bogus Rim area. Marked on the map are Bogus Creek Falls, and just south of the falls is Bogus Creek Cave. On the bail out track is Bogus Lake. All are worth exploring. This is a lengthy and difficult ride through the lava fields, with rocky trails, sharp lava, difficult route finding and spectacular views. There is a bail out that will cut over 15 miles off of the loop if gas or time becomes an issue. There are many other tracks available to those willing to expose themselves to the distance and time required. This area could be targeted for overnight trips easily. Opposite the mouth of Bogus Creek at the Owyhee River is the China Garden, a wild landscape of hanging plateaus and outrageous rock cliffs. Ranches were settled along Bogus Creek before the turn of the century. Turning off at Bogus Ranch will steer you down to one original site. Some of the original sites still have buildings on them. Bogus Lake was a well-known location for riders to corral and break horses. The creek was named after a group of riders counting on water found it dry and proclaimed it "a bogus".

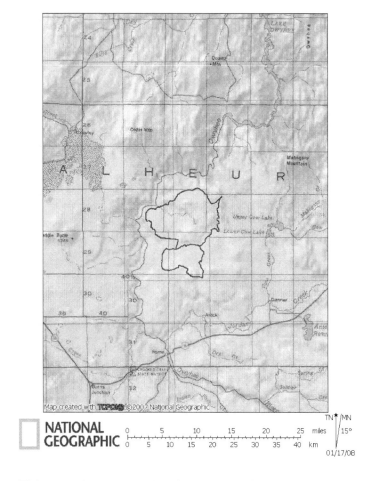

This area became quite developed after the Bannock War of 1878 and ranches and settlers descended on the region. Jordan Creek, Cow Creek, Bogus Creek, and Crooked Creek all became developed ranches. The Crossing of the Owyhee (Rome) was a focal point of this area, and native people have crossed here for over 10,000 years.

Area 2 Route 12 – Cow Lakes

Topo 7.5" series: Jordan Valley, OR ID, Antelope Reservoir, OR, Cow Lakes, OR, Jordan Craters South, OR, Bogus Bench, OR, Lambert Rocks, OR, Arock, OR, Threemile Hill, OR, Danner, OR
Grade IV
Difficulty: Difficult (100+ mi.), route finding, and terrain.
Route Start: Jordan Valley 42°58'26" N, 117°03'11" W
Length of route: 93 mile loop
Starting coords: 42°58'26" N, 117°03'11" W
Finish coords: Same

Route description:

42°58'26" N, 117°03'11" W
→ 42°59'18" N, 117°08'56" W
→ 42°59'09" N, 117°11'54" W
← 42°59'35" N, 117°12'40" W
← 43°01'08" N, 117°16'30" W
→ 43°01'33" N, 117°17'14" W
→ 43°02'40" N, 117°17'52" W
← 43°03'13" N, 117°17'24" W
← 43°04'33" N, 117°17'45" W
← 43°04'54" N, 117°17'34" W
← 43°05'22" N, 117°19'04" W
→ 43°04'27" N, 117°18'37" W
→ 43°02'36" N, 117°19'33" W
→ 43°02'26" N, 117°21'01" W
→ 43°03'40" N, 117°22'51" W

← 43°05'23" N, 117°30'05" W
← 43°05'05" N, 117°30'04" W
↑ 43°04'26" N, 117°30'51" W
→ 43°03'24" N, 117°32'11" W
→ 43°03'23" N, 117°34'24" W
* ← Bogus Lake & Corrals
← 43°02'59" N, 117°36'12" W
← 43°03'07" N, 117°37'51" W
← 43°02'24" N, 117°38'29" W
↑ 43°01'18" N, 117°38'35" W
→ 43°00'34" N, 117°38'29" W
↑ 42°59'23" N, 117°37'48" W
← 42°58'43" N, 117°37'02" W
→ 42°56'39" N, 117°34'05" W
→ 42°56'37" N, 117°32'18" W
← 42°55'46" N, 117°33'32" W
← 42°55'20" N, 117°33'32" W
← 42°54'53" N, 117°31'31" W
→ 42°55'13" N, 117°24'20" W
* ← Dixons' Rock & Holdup Rock
42°55'32" N, 117°24'44" W
* Charbonneau Gravesite
→ 42°57'32" N, 117°19'47" W
→ 42°57'32" N, 117°17'57" W
→ 42°58'13" N, 117°13'30" W
← 42°57'56" N, 117°11'00" W
42°58'26" N, 117°03'11" W Jordan Valley

Starting in Jordan Valley, OR, and exploring the southern lava fields, Cow Lakes, portions of Bogus Bench, through Hidden Valley, Arock, Arock dam, Jordan Creek, the grave of Jean Baptiste Charbonneau, Sacajewea's son, and finally back to Jordan Valley. Another lengthy and difficult ride in the desert.

Steve Silva

The Arock, Danner, and Lower Jordan Creek communities are steeped in history. The lush Jordan Creek Valley has been traveled and used by native peoples for tens of thousands of years. Indians fished for salmon in the Jordan, and Indian writings are on local rocks. This is the original immigrant trail, following the north side of Jordan Creek.

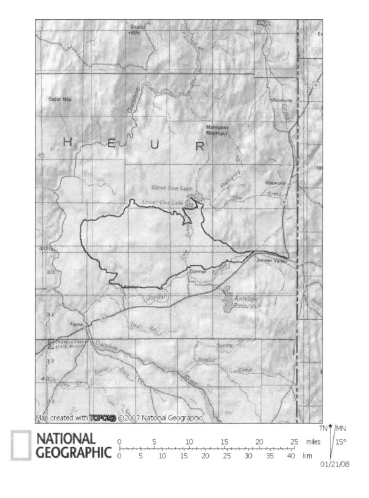

This area is relatively unknown, and when US Highway 95 was routed to its present location, these small towns and historical areas were lost and forgotten to the general populace. The Jordan Creek Valley is a wonderful reminder of a time past. Seek it out, you will enjoy what you find.

Area 1 Route 13 – Jump Creek

Topo 7.5" series:
Jump Creek Canyon, ID
Grade II
Difficulty: Moderate. There are some short steep rocky stretches.
Route Start: Jump Creek 43°30'07" N, 116°54'36" W
Length of route: 21 mile loop
Starting coords: 43°30'07" N, 116°54'36" W
Finish coords: Same

Route description:

43°30'07" N, 116°54'36" W
→ 43°29'43" N, 116°54'36" W
← 43°29'41" N, 116°54'49" W
→ 43°28'59" N, 116°55'22" W
→ 43°27'46" N, 116°56'22" W
← 43°27'12" N, 116°57'23" W
← 43°26'30" N, 116°58'47" W
← 43°25'56" N, 116°58'55" W
→ 43°25'55" N, 116°58'01" W
← 43°24'06" N, 116°56'49" W
← 43°23'56" N, 116°55'11" W
← 43°24'16" N, 116°54'13" W

French John cutoff:

→ 43°24'16" N, 116°54'13" W
Summit: 43°24'50" N, 116°52'50" W
→ 43°25'42" N, 116°54'35" W
← 43°26'25" N, 116°54'23" W
← 43°29'02" N, 116°54'32" W
← 43°29'33" N, 116°54'32" W
← 43°29'38" N, 116°54'30" W

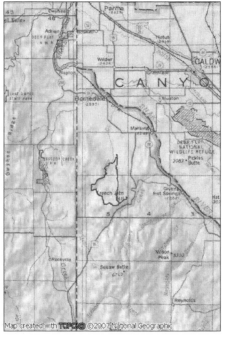

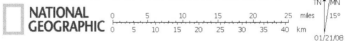

NATIONAL GEOGRAPHIC

Jump Creek Falls is a well-known destination outside of Marsing, ID. The waterfall is a short but spectacular hike upstream and should not be missed. Trails

abound all around the canyon, and the canyon rim offers incredible views. Poison Oak fills the canyon bottoms in the summer. Up top near the headwaters wild
horses roam freely. This access can link with Poison
Creek, Sands Basin, Strodes Basin, and ultimately
Succor Creek Canyon. The French John hill has a
marked grave of Charlie Brown, victim of a local gun-
fight hidden in the draw.

Area 1 Route 14 – Poison Creek – Sands Basin

Topo 7.5" series:
Jump Creek Canyon, ID, Piute Butte, ID
Grade II
Difficulty: Easy.
Route Start: Jump Creek 43°30'07" N, 116°54'36" W
Length of route: 17 miles to Hwy 95
Starting coords: 43°30'07" N, 116°54'36" W
Finish coords: 43°20'49" N, 116°56'53" W

Route description:

43°30'07" N, 116°54'36" W

Poison Creek Stage Station

43°30'10" N, 116°56'15" W
← 43°29'49" N, 116°57'26" W
← 43°29'03" N, 116°58'31" W
↑ 43°26'30" N, 116°58'47" W
→ 43°25'55" N, 116°58'56" W
← 43°25'36" N, 116°58'54" W
← 43°25'07" N, 116°59'04" W
→ 43°24'49" N, 116°59'04" W

→ 43°22'37" N, 116°59'56" W
← 43°21'53" N, 116°59'50" W
↑ 43°20'56" N, 116°57'22" W
43°20'49" N, 116°56'53" W

Jump Creek is bordered to the Northwest by Poison Creek canyon, a more intense and remote slot canyon. Named for its namesake plant, the canyon is only slightly accessible. A relatively well maintained road

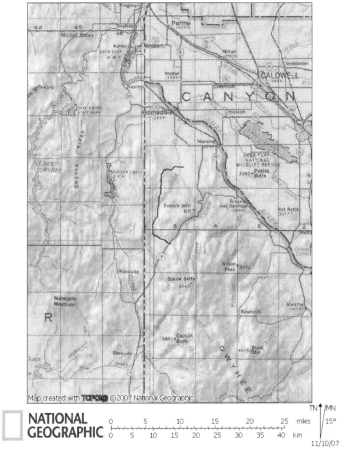

Map created with TOPO! ©2007 National Geographic

NATIONAL GEOGRAPHIC

| | 0 | 5 | 10 | 15 | 20 | 25 | miles |
| | 0 | 5 | 10 | 15 | 20 | 25 | 30 | 35 | 40 | km |

TN ↑ /MN
15°
11/10/07

takes the grade all the way to the rim and traverses through Sands Basin to intersect with Hwy 95. Access to Strodes Basin, and ultimately Succor Creek is also available. A word of wisdom; stay off this stretch of desert in wet or muddy conditions. Sands Basin is famous for its Owyhee gumbo. The Stage Station has really fallen into disrepair in the last years. It was still being used as a home well into the 1980's.

Area 1 Route 15 – Poison Creek – Strodes Basin

Topo 7.5" series:
Jump Creek Canyon, ID, Pole Creek Top, OR ID
Grade II
Difficulty: Moderate with a very technical, steep and rocky descent/ascent into Strodes Basin/Pond. (Can be by passed to the North)
Route Start: Jump Creek 43°30'07" N, 116°54'36" W
Length of route: 7 miles to Strodes; 16 miles to Succor Creek State Park
Starting coords: 43°30'07" N, 116°54'36" W
Finish coords: 43°29'36" N, 117°00'19" W

Route description:

43°30'07" N, 116°54'36" W

Poison Creek Stage Station

43°30'10" N, 116°56'15" W
→ 43°29'03" N, 116°58'31" W
← 43°29'28" N, 116°59'03" W start of steep technical descent
43°29'38" N, 117°00'02" W Strodes Basin/Pond

43°29'36" N, 117°00'19" W
← 43°29'51" N, 117°00'37" W
← 43°29'56" N, 117°02'38" W
← 43°30'03" N, 117°03'19" W
↑ 43°27'34" N, 117°06'51" W
Succor Creek State Park.
43°27'13" N, 117°07'13" W

Strodes Basin/Pond is a small pond situated in a remote canyon. The arrival is abrupt as the descent liter-
ally falls off the face of the table's rim. The descent is
technical, rocky, and steep. Coming back out is much
more of a rodeo than the ride in. Eagles aeries are
found in the high cliff walls. Upland game birds and

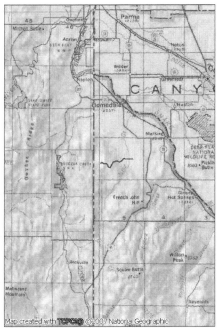

Get Lost! Adventure Tours in the Owyhee Desert

waterfowl use the pond frequently and evenings and mornings are filled with the calls of Chukar, ducks, and quail. The pond also allows access to Succor Creek via Antelope Springs, and back to Graveyard Point to the North.

Area 3 Route 16 – Sommer-camp Rd - Shares Basin

Topo 7.5" series:
Opalene Gulch, ID, Soldier Cap, ID, Piute Butte, ID, Captain Butte, ID
Grade III
Difficulty: Moderate
Route Start: Approx. 5 miles from Marsing on Hwy 78
Length of route: 24 miles to McBride Creek junction.
Starting coords: 43°28'24" N, 116°46'54" W
Finish coords: 43°14'39" N, 116°54'21" W

Route description:

43°28'24" N, 116°46'54" W
→ 43°25'48" N, 116°46'56" W
↑ 43°25'36" N, 116°47'21" W
← 43°24'59" N, 116°47'57" W
← 43°24'55" N, 116°47'59" W
→ 43°24'14" N, 116°48'28" W
→ 43°23'22" N, 116°49'21" W
→ 43°23'03" N, 116°49'22" W
↑ 43°22'52" N, 116°50'03" W
→ 43°22'49" N, 116°50'16" W
→ 43°22'35" N, 116°50'47" W
← 43°21'52" N, 116°51'43" W

← 43°21'46" N, 116°51'40" W
→ 43°21'29" N, 116°51'25" W
→ 43°19'39" N, 116°53'04" W
→ 43°19'43" N, 116°54'56" W
← 43°19'27" N, 116°55'15" W
→ 43°18'05" N, 116°55'02" W
→ 43°16'38" N, 116°54'03" W
← 43°15'28" N, 116°54'00" W
→ 43°15'19" N, 116°53'54" W
McBride Creek junction.
43°14'39" N, 116°54'21" W

Sommercamp Rd. bisects the leading edge of the Ow-yhee Mountains just outside of Marsing, ID. The road runs from Hwy 78 to Hwy 95 and provides access to a unique and seldom visited areas filled with wild hors-es. The upper reaches of Squaw Creek Canyon are reached via Shares as well. Joining up with McBride Creek, it then opens up many routes that ultimately bring the northern area above Reynolds Creek into access. Many line shacks and old homesteads are hidden in the tight canyons. Respect private property, and remember to leave gates as you find them. Roads and trail intersections are vague and often maps are not accurate as they traverse the basin. Be patient and adjust your travel directions accordingly. Again, this is not a place to be during wet or muddy conditions. Squaw Butte summit; turn **LEFT** at 43°15'19" N, 116°53'54" W

Area 3 Route 17 – Wilson Creek

Topo 7.5" series:
Wilson Peak, ID, Soldier Cap, ID, Rooster Comb Peak, ID, Captain Butte, ID, Piute Butte, ID
Grade III
Difficulty: Moderate, good route finding skills needed
Route Start: Hwy 78 aprox.16 miles from Marsing, ID
Length of route: aprox 32 miles
Starting coords: 43°21'42" N, 116°39'13" W
Finish coords: 43°20'08" N, 116°57'31" W

Route description:

43°21'42" N, 116°39'13" W
→ 43°21'20" N, 116°42'04" W
→ 43°19'06" N, 116°45'39" W
← 43°18'31" N, 116°46'28" W
← 43°18'20" N, 116°46'20" W
→ 43°17'23" N, 116°46'42" W
← 43°17'16" N, 116°47'11" W

→ 43°16'41" N, 116°47'39" W multiple routes; typical route will follow Salmon Creek up.

→ 43°16'59" N, 116°49'16" W

← 43°17'06" N, 116°49'18" W

↑ 43°16'00" N, 116°50'59" W

→ 43°15'43" N, 116°50'56" W

← 43°15'11" N, 116°52'02" W

← 43°14'40" N, 116°51'58" W

→ 43°13'56" N, 116°52'29" W

← 43°14'00" N, 116°52'38" W

→ 43°14'05" N, 116°53'21" W

← 43°14'39" N, 116°54'24" W

→ 43°15'06" N, 116°56'28" W

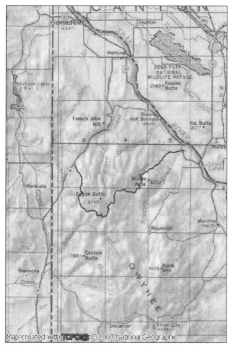

→ 43°16'55" N, 116°56'38" W
→ 43°17'03" N, 116°56'38" W
→ 43°18'06" N, 116°56'28" W
← 43°18'34" N, 116°56'26" W
43°20'08" N, 116°57'31" W

Wilson Creek road is a major access point off of Hwy 78. In general the route traverses the Owyhee range to the west and ends up on Hwy 95. Following Wilson Creek, then Salmon Creek, and finally Cottonwood Creek, the route ends up on the McBride Creek/Sands Basin road, which takes you to Hwy 95. Many routes bisect this trail. Be aware and don't be afraid to explore other directions.

Area 3 Route 18 – Chipmunk Meadow

Topo 7.5" series:
Rooster Comb Peak, ID, Reynolds, ID
Grade III
Difficulty: Moderate, good route finding skills necessary
Route Start: Either via McBride Creek (Route 17) or Reynolds Creek (43°12'08" N, 116°44'57" W)
Length of route: aprox 12 miles
Starting coords: 43°12'08" N, 116°44'57" W (Reynolds ID.) Or 43°13'55" N, 116°52'26" W (Cottonwood Creek)
Finish coords: Same

Route description:

43°13'55" N, 116°52'26" W
→ 43°11'45" N, 116°51'34" W

← 43°10'55" N, 116°51'23" W
→ 43°10'51" N, 116°49'51" W
→ 43°11'01" N, 116°49'22" W
← 43°10'57" N, 116°48'34" W
← 43°10'57" N, 116°48'04" W
→ 43°11'01" N, 116°48'01" W
← 43°11'49" N, 116°46'11" W
← 43°11'54" N, 116°44'57" W
43°12'08" N, 116°44'57" W

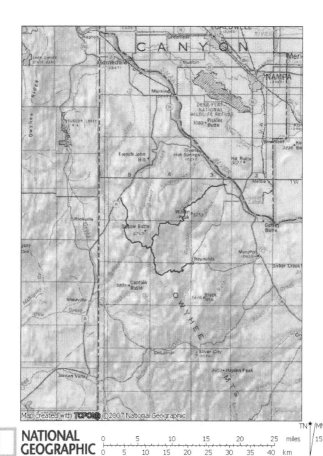

Chipmunk is a classic Owyhee Mountain location. Beautiful setting with both modern cattle operations and historic marks left upon the land. The route is accessible from either Reynolds Creek or from Hwy 95 and McBride Creek. Tread lightly and enjoy. The Chipmunk name came from the early settler in the area who was described as a small man who dressed neatly and was quick on his feet. He was rumored to be a ladies man and was a regular dance attendee.

Mildretta Adams described him thus in her book "Owyhee Cattlemen", Owyhee Publishing, Homedale Idaho, which is an absolute treasure of information and unbelievable pictures from the early days of the Owyhee. This book and many others are available through the Owyhee Historical Society in Murphy.

Area 3 Route 19 – Reynolds Area

Slacks Mt. – Silver City

Topo 7.5" series: Walters Butte, ID, Wilson Peak, ID, Reynolds, ID, Silver City, ID
Grade III
Difficulty: Difficult, with steep rocky and washed out sections.
Route Start: Hwy 78, aprox 1 mile from Walters Ferry Bridge
Length of route: aprox 35 miles
Starting coords: 43°19'44" N, 116°36'12" W
Finish coords: 43°00'51" N, 116°43'53" W

Route description:

43°19'44" N, 116°36'12" W
Follow the road to Reynolds,
← 43°12'08" N, 116°44'58" W
→ 43°11'58" N, 116°42'50" W Slacks Mountain OHV
   parking area.
← 43°11'43" N, 116°43'00" W
* ← **43°08'53" N, 116°42'39" W for difficult section over Black Mt.**
* → **For easier road to Slacks Corner cutoff.**

Following route is for Black Mt.

← 43°07'08" N, 116°43'00" W
→ 43°07'01" N, 116°42'59" W
→ 43°06'52" N, 116°42'59" W
← 43°06'31" N, 116°43'19" W
→ 43°06'02" N, 116°43'07" W
→ 43°05'14" N, 116°43'46" W

Slacks Corner Junction 43°04'58" N, 116°44'30" W

← 43°04'26" N, 116°44'47" W
← 43°04'04" N, 116°44'44" W
→ 43°03'51" N, 116°44'37" W
← 43°03'30" N, 116°44'34" W
→ 43°02'54" N, 116°44'04" W
→ 43°02'09" N, 116°43'18" W New York Summit
→ 43°01'38" N, 116°43'23" W
← 43°01'33" N, 116°43'59" W
Silver City 43°00'51" N, 116°43'53" W

The classic route to Silver City. There are actually many variables, but this main route can be made substantially easier by heading to Slacks Corner, and not taking the Black Mountain trail. This route (Black Mountain) has some very steep, very rough, very rocky sections to tackle. The connection at Slacks Corner will bypass much of the rougher areas. Spectacular vistas of the high mountain meadows and tree-lined slopes of the Owyhee Mountains make this trail by far one of the most popular routes to Silver City. Even with many users, the trail is a wonderful and classic trip. Special

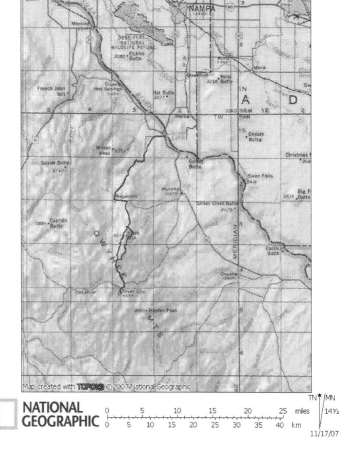

Map created with TOPO!® ©2007 National Geographic

NATIONAL GEOGRAPHIC

| 0 | 5 | 10 | 15 | 20 | 25 | miles |
| 0 | 5 | 10 | 15 | 20 | 25 | 30 | 35 | 40 | km |

TN⌖/MN
14½
11/17/07

areas are Bull Meadow, Avondale Basin, Sheepherder Spring, New York Summit, and the famous mining town of Silver City.

The Owyhee Front is an immensely popular area and is frequented by large amounts of ATV and OHV users. The area is constantly under scrutiny by many, including BLM and private landowners. Be sure to follow all applicable rules and regulations in this area. In addition, we should contact our representatives with opinions and suggestions for keeping existing routes and trails open for use. There is a movement to begin shutting down many trails and roads that have historically been available to us all. Stay informed and become a voice for the continued use of our trails. Send letters emails and talk to officials in the field while riding. Be PROACTIVE before its too late.

War Eagle and Hayden Peak are reached by turning at 43°01'38" N, 116°43'23" W and following the ridge south.

Area 3 Route 20 – Murphy - Tiddie Springs

Topo 7.5" series:
Murphy, ID, Reynolds, ID, Silver City, ID
Grade III
Difficulty: Moderate
Route Start: Murphy, ID
Length of route: aprox 26 miles
Starting coords: 43°13'15" N, 116°33'20" W
Finish coords: Same

Route description:

43°13'15" N, 116°33'20" W
→ 43°12'27" N, 116°33'47" W
Follow the Reynolds road to the BLM sign for Tiddie
  Springs.
← 43°11'23" N, 116°38'39" W
← 43°10'59" N, 116°39'22" W
→ 43°07'01" N, 116°41'20" W
← 43°06'48" N, 116°41'26" W
← 43°06'09" N, 116°40'04" W
→ 43°06'24" N, 116°39'37" W
← 43°06'31" N, 116°39'28" W

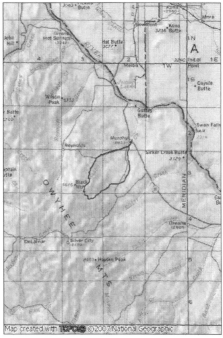

→ 43°06'37" N, 116°39'20" W
← 43°07'01" N, 116°38'37" W
→ 43°07'55" N, 116°36'08" W
← 43°08'14" N, 116°34'42" W, junction with the Silver
  City road.
← 43°08'54" N, 116°34'11" W
→ 43°09'17" N, 116°33'53" W
→ 43°11'11" N, 116°34'00" W
43°12'27" N, 116°33'46" W

A great and scenic loop that starts in the historic town of Murphy, the Owyhee County seat. The Owyhee Historical Society is headquartered here.

The display and historical items to view are simply astounding. Books and information are for sale and provide priceless knowledge. The Tiddie Springs loop takes a path that winds up and through rocky canyons, timbered slopes, and incredible granite spires. Cabins and line shacks dot the trail, and one cabin is wall papered with historic newspaper (check out the box scores for the early New York Yankees!). Tiddie Springs pours out of a metal pipe with gusto. Not to be missed Diamond Basin, Point of Rocks Springs and the granite outcroppings that surround it as you near the Silver City road, culminating back at the starting point of Murphy.

Area 3   Route 21 – Triangle

Topo 7.5" series: Oreana, ID, Antelope Spring, ID, Toy
  Pass, ID, Triangle Reservoir, ID, Triangle Flat, ID,
  Combination Ridge, ID, Flint, ID, Stonehouse Creek,
  ID, Jordan Valley, OR ID

Grade III
Difficulty: Easy
Route Start: Oreana, ID aprox 44 miles from Marsing, ID.
Length of route: aprox 57 miles
Starting coords: 43°04'20" N, 116°23'29" W
Finish coords: Jordan Valley, OR. 42°58'26" N, 117°03'12" W

Route description:

43°04'20" N, 116°23'29" W
→ 43°02'22" N, 116°23'42" W
Toy Pass
42°54'14" N, 116°32'48" W
→ 42°51'05" N, 116°36'04" W
→ 42°48'47" N, 116°38'22" W
* Triangle and Triangle Reservoir
← 42°48'47" N, 116°38'22" W
(42°48'13" N, 116°38'06" W. Antelope Ridge Rd. access)
(Triangle 42°47'01" N, 116°37'31" W)
← 42°53'36" N, 116°48'25" W
(→Flint Creek access)
↑ 42°55'25" N, 116°59'49" W
42°58'26" N, 117°03'12" W

A terrific route! Relatively good roads through the central Owyhee Mountains will give you a fine tour. Starting in the old town of Oreana (don't miss the pioneer cemetery!) and then travel the Triangle road over the famous Bachman Grade, Toy Pass and down to Triangle Flat where Triangle is reached via a short side spur. Continue on to Jordan Valley by way of North Boulder Creek, Flint Creek, and finally Jordan Creek

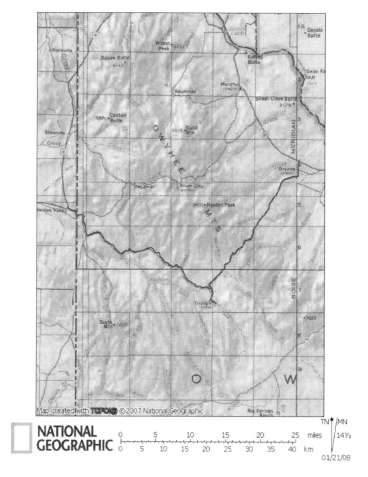

before reaching Pleasant Valley, and finally Jordan Valley. Many side trips are possible using this route as a primary east to west artery.

Area 3 Route 22 – Antelope Ridge Rd.

Topo 7.5" series: Oreana, ID, Antelope Spring, ID, Toy
  Pass, ID, Triangle Reservoir, ID, Hurry Up Creek, ID,
  Clover Mountain, ID
Grade III
Difficulty: Moderate
Route Start: Oreana, ID aprox 44 miles from Marsing,
  ID
Length of route: aprox 43 miles
Starting coords: 43°04'20" N, 116°23'29" W
Finish coords: Mud Flat Rd. 42°38'55" N, 116°27'32" W

Route description:

43°04'20" N, 116°23'29" W
→ 43°02'22" N, 116°23'42" W
Toy Pass
42°54'14" N, 116°32'48" W
→ 42°51'05" N, 116°36'04" W
→ 42°48'47" N, 116°38'22" W
← 42°48'13" N, 116°38'06" W
→ 42°48'02" N, 116°36'56" W
→ 27,42°47'24" N, 116°35'45" W
→ 42°44'49" N, 116°31'38" W
← 42°43'35" N, 116°31'01" W
↑ 42°42'34" N, 116°30'15" W
(* ← Juniper Station 1 mile aprox.
→ 42°42'55" N, 116°29'47" W
← 42°42'50" N, 116°29'39" W
42°42'55" N, 116°29'36" W)
← 42°40'07" N, 116°28'28" W
← 42°39'00" N, 116°27'38" W
42°38'55" N, 116°27'32" W

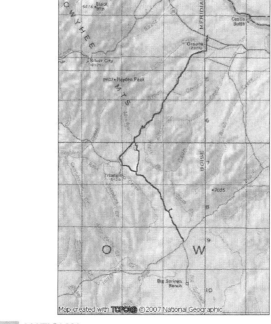

NATIONAL GEOGRAPHIC

Another obscure route that bisects a lonely stretch of the Owyhee Mountains. Intersecting with the Mud Flat Rd, you can then either end up in Jordan Valley, or Grandview. Take the short side trip to Juniper Station and check out the old site. Many routes break off of this road so plan accordingly.

Area 3 Route 23 – South Mountain

Topo 7.5" series: Jordan Valley, OR ID, Stonehouse
   Creek, ID, Williams Creek, ID, Cliffs, ID
Grade III

Difficulty: Easy
Route Start: Jordan Valley, OR
Length of route: aprox 21 miles to the summit look-
   out.
Starting coords: 42°58'27" N, 117°03'12" W
Finish coords: 42°44'24" N, 116°54'51" W

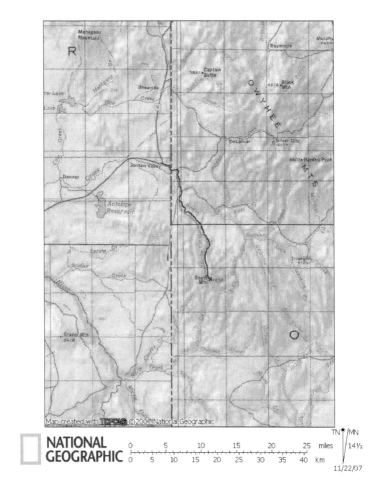

Route description:

42°58'27" N, 117°03'12" W
← 42°52'47" N, 116°59'12" W
→ 42°49'48" N, 116°55'44" W
→ 42°48'36" N, 116°55'00" W
← 42°47'16" N, 116°55'50" W
→ 42°44'47" N, 116°54'45" W
South Mountain Lookout
42°44'24" N, 116°54'51" W

South Mountain is one of the high points of the Ow-yhee Mountains. A lookout perched on top gives access to superb views in all directions. Many mines dot the surrounding hillsides, and the snow is sometimes blocking the trail into the early summer. Take the Mud Flat road out of Jordan Valley, and look for the BLM signs that direct you up Williams Creek and the obvious switchbacks to the summit. From South Mountain you can loop back in almost all directions and hit one of the main roads or trails that will take you back to either the west or east side of the range.

Area 3 Route 24 – Indian Meadows

Topo 7.5" series: Jordan Valley, OR ID, Stonehouse
    Creek, ID, Williams Creek, ID, Combination Ridge,
    ID, Indian Meadows, ID, Fairylawn, ID, Cliffs, ID, Ju-
    niper Point, OR ID, Parsnip Peak, OR ID
Grade IV
Difficulty: Moderate with difficult route finding and
    some rough trail.
Route Start: Jordan Valley, OR
Length of route: aprox 70 mile loop

Get Lost! Adventure Tours in the Owyhee Desert

Starting coords: 42°58'27" N, 117°03'12" W
Finish coords: Same

Route description:

42°58'27" N, 117°03'12" W
← 42°54'09" N, 117°00'08" W
← 42°48'36" N, 116°55'01" W
Mill Creek 42°44'59" N, 116°51'37" W
← 42°43'37" N, 116°50'56" W
← 42°42'02" N, 116°49'58" W
→ 42°41'52" N, 116°48'41" W
→ 42°41'44" N, 116°48'29" W

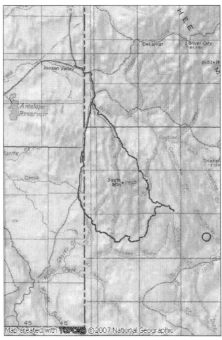

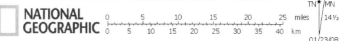

*← Indian Meadows Springs turnoff
→ 42°41'08" N, 116°46'34" W
Indian Meadows Springs
42°41'01" N, 116°46'26" W
→ 42°37'53" N, 116°51'23" W
→ 42°37'24" N, 116°52'26" W
→ 42°37'36" N, 116°56'35" W
← 42°38'01" N, 116°57'24" W
→ 42°38'04" N, 116°57'38" W
← 42°38'22" N, 116°58'07" W
Junction with Mud Flat Rd.
→ 42°38'22" N, 116°58'52" W
42°58'27" N, 117°03'12" W

Indian Meadows is at the headwaters of Nip and Tuck creek, and was a primary summer camping area for the local Indians. Incredible terrain, beautiful juniper forests and a tougher than average route make this great loop very desirable. There are routes not on maps that will take you to alternate connection points. Explore the area around Indian Meadow Springs. Begin in Jordan Valley. At Pleasant Valley School, the route heads up Williams Creek, leaving it at the South Mt. turn off. After Mill Creek, follow the trail up and into the higher elevations of Noon Creek, and finally Indian Meadows, Indian Meadows Springs, and Nip and Tuck Creek.

Area 3 Route 25 – Murphy to Silver City Area

Silver City – War Eagle and Cinnabar peaks

Topo 7.5" series: Murphy, ID, Sinker Canyon, ID, Silver City, ID, Cinnabar Mountain, ID
Grade III
Difficulty: Easy
Route Start: Hwy 78, aprox 4.5 mile from Murphy ID.
Length of route: aprox 25 miles
Starting coords: 43°09'30" N, 116°30'31" W
Finish coords: 43°00'54" N, 116°43'52" W

Route description:

43°09'30" N, 116°30'31" W
→ 43°04'49" N, 116°36'39" W Side trip to over look a section of Sinker Creek Canyon
43°03'52" N, 116°38'04" W crossing Sinker Creek
→ 43°02'09" N, 116°40'54" W
* ← **To Sinker Tunnel @ 43°01'08" N, 116°40'47" W**
43°01'08" N, 116°40'47" W New York Summit
→ 43°01'08" N, 116°40'47" W
* ← **To War Eagle and Cinnabar**
← 43°01'33" N, 116°43'58" W
43°01'33" N, 116°43'58" W

South of Murphy along Highway 78 is the sign for Silver City, perhaps Idaho's most famous Ghost Town. Established between 1863-1865 with the discovery of gold and silver, it became a rallying point for miners and settlers alike. It became the county seat in 1866 and held that distinction until 1935. Remote, rough, and raw, the town was home to as many as 2,500 inhabitants with multiple town sites up and down Jordan Creek and the Silver City Mountains. This road takes you up through the desert flatlands, crosses Sinker Creek, and finally climbs to New York Summit before descending to Jordan Creek and into Silver. Side trips to War Eagle and Cinnabar will take you past numerous mines, homesteads and historical locations. Make sure to check out the After Thought Mine, Fairview Cemetery, the Oro Fino and the Bluejacket Mine to name a few. There are many side trips available in this area. Within Silver City itself is a lifetime of historical buildings and sights. The hotel, school, church and other sites are open to the public at certain times of

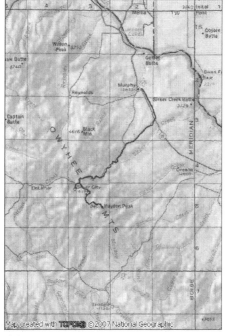

the year. The Owyhee Historical Society in Murphy is a treasure trove of books and other information to the interested individual.

Area 3 Route 26 - Cow Creek-
De Lamar-Silver City

Topo 7.5" series: Sheaville, OR ID, Swisher Mountain, ID, De Lamar, ID, Silver City, ID
Grade III
Difficulty: Moderate
Route Start: Hwy 95, aprox 12 mile from Jordan Valley
Length of route: aprox 25 miles
Starting coords: 43°08'08" N, 117°02'47" W
Finish coords: 43°00'54" N, 116°43'52" W

Route description:

43°08'08" N, 117°02'47" W
→ 43°08'10" N, 117°01'57" W
← 43°07'45" N, 117°02'12" W
← 43°03'38" N, 116°56'37" W
→ 43°01'21" N, 116°51'47" W
← 43°01'30" N, 116°51'09" W
De Lamar site
43°01'19" N, 116°49'34" W
→ 43°01'33" N, 116°43'58" W
43°00'54" N, 116°43'52" W

The route from the Jordan Valley side of the Owyhee Mountains starts about a dozen miles before Jordan Valley, and follows Cow Creek to Jordan Creek, and then proceeds past De Lamar and into Silver. Soon after starting the route you will pass Camp Lyons (43°07'42" N, 117°01'40" W), just north of the road before you cross the Oregon Idaho border. This military fort was home to a contingent of Calvary tasked with keeping the Indians managed and the white miners and settlers protected as well as a stronghold on the emigrant trail. Many skirmishes and running battles were fought before white inhabitants ultimately settled the area. All along Jordan Creek old mines, homesteads and signs of mining activities can be observed. Present day mining and claims are still being worked, so respect the private property signs. The Silver City Cemetery can be seen just as you enter town on the

far side of the creek. It is well worth visiting to see the names and read the history of these brave pioneers. The area is a vast and hardy testament to the lure of gold and the riches many dreamed of. Silver City has been called the "Queen of Idaho Ghost Towns".

Silver City's hilltop Catholic Church.

Area 3 Route 27 – Flint

Topo 7.5" series: Silver City, ID, Flint, ID, Stonehouse Creek, ID, Jordan Valley, OR ID
Grade IV
Difficulty: Moderate
Route Start: Silver City
Length of route: aprox 32 miles to Jordan Valley, OR.
Starting coords: 43°01'02" N, 116°43'57" W
Finish coords: 42°58'26" N, 117°03'11" W

Route description:

43°01'02" N, 116°43'57" W
→ 43°00'18" N, 116°43'46" W
← 42°59'06" N, 116°45'21" W
* → **access to Florida Mt. views**
↑ 42°58'37" N, 116°45'52" W
* ← **Access to Hayden Peak area**
← 42°57'25" N, 116°47'16" W

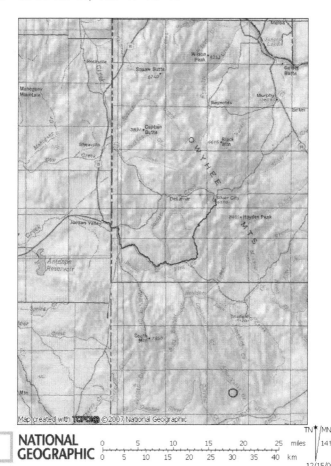

Map created with TOPO!® ©2007 National Geographic

NATIONAL
GEOGRAPHIC

0 5 10 15 20 25 miles
0 5 10 15 20 25 30 35 40 km

TN MN
14½
12/15/07

Flint site
42°55'09" N, 116°47'07" W
→ 42°53'36" N, 116°48'25" W
* ← Access to Triangle Rd.
→ 42°55'30" N, 116°59'49" W
42°58'26" N, 117°03'11" W

The mining town of Flint was one of the earliest camps in the Owyhee Mountains. It is estimated that between 1860 and 1870 close to 1,500 miners called Flint home. Discoveries of tin, cinnabar and gold led to the areas growth. A post office was stationed here from 1892 – 1914. This route starts from Silver, and continues on to Jordan Valley. Flint can be looped through from various points, and can also be accessed via the Triangle Rd.

One of my favorite loops is to combine the peaks of War Eagle, Cinnabar (Hayden), and finally Flint on my way back to Silver and then finally home via Murphy.

Area 3 Route 28 – Mud Flat Road overview

The Mud Flat Road

Topo 7.5" series: Jordan Valley, OR ID, Stonehouse Creek, ID, Parsnip Peak, OR ID, Juniper Point, OR ID, Cliffs, ID, Fairylawn, ID, Pleasant Valley, ID, Slack Mountain, ID, Wagon Box Basin, ID, Big Springs Ranch, ID, Clover Mountain, ID, Snow Creek, ID, Rough Mountain, ID, Purjue Canyon, ID, Chalk Hills, ID, Grand View, ID
Grade IV

Difficulty: Easy, well maintained, but long
Route Start: Jordan Valley, OR
Length of route: aprox 110 miles to Grandview ID
Starting coords: 42°58'27" N, 117°03'12" W
Finish coords: 42°59'00" N, 116°05'50" W

Mud Flat Road is a landmark ride. This road is des-ignated the Owyhee Uplands National Backcountry Byway, and is the gateway to enough remote and ad-venturesome rides to last a lifetime. After 25 years I still have barely scratched its surface. Traversing from Jordan Valley to Grandview it bisects the heart of the Owyhee Mountains. With the Silver City Mountains to the North, and the Canyonlands to the South, fuel, permission, and your own desire to explore are the only limits. I can't emphasize enough the importance of getting permission to cross private land in these ar-eas. Historically this land is rich with stories of desper-adoes, horse thieves, Indian battles, river crossings and cattle drives, horse breaking and other tall tales. Seek the heart of the "The Big Quiet" and you will not be disappointed. This road is really the main artery of the Owyhees'.

Another fine source of fantastic information about this road and area is found at: http://www.hikeidaho.com/desertbk/owyheeco/dodrmu/dodrmu.html. This is a free but copyrighted site and is well worth looking at. In addition to the standard route description I will also add a short note for routes that branch off of the Mud Flat Rd. to help with planning other excursions.

Route description:

42°58'27" N, 117°03'12" W
→ 42°57'40" N, 117°00'24" W (1)
→ 42°55'26" N, 116°59'49" W (2)
→ 42°54'09" N, 117°00'08" W (3)
42°48'13" N, 117°01'37" W (4)
← 42°41'57" N, 117°02'09" W (5)
42°39'26" N, 117°00'11" W (6)
42°38'21" N, 116°58'52" W (7)
42°35'30" N, 116°58'53" W (8)
42°34'15" N, 116°59'13" W (9)
42°33'03" N, 116°58'22" W (10)
42°31'02" N, 116°53'39" W (11)
42°32'25" N, 116°48'17" W (12)
42°34'21" N, 116°44'08" W (13)
42°34'53" N, 116°40'34" W (14)
42°34'52" N, 116°39'55" W (15)
42°36'13" N, 116°33'21" W (16)
42°38'54" N, 116°27'34" W (17)
42°41'02" N, 116°25'29" W (18)
42°41'27" N, 116°24'23" W (19)
42°42'33" N, 116°22'15" W (20)
42°44'23" N, 116°18'50" W (21)
42°47'53" N, 116°13'45" W (22)
42°51'07" N, 116°05'29" W (23)
Grandview, ID
42°59'00" N, 116°05'50" W

1. The road to Wagontown and the De Lamar mine area.
2. Access road to Triangle.
3. Pleasant Valley creek and Indian Meadows access.
4. Lone Tree Ranch site and Lone Tree Creek.

5. Three Forks access road.
6. Dougal reservoir and Dougal Ranch site.
7. Cliffs, and access to Indian Meadows.
8. North Fork of the Owyhee campground.
9. Fairylawn, old way station for stage line, and post office. Named for the small greenery watered by windmill from spring.
10. Access to the Lowrey Ranch, Circle Bar ranch, and backdoor to Three Forks.
11. Hanley cabin access. Payne cabin road, access to Crutcher's Crossing on the Owyhee.
12. Grasshopper Trail access.
13. Indian Battleground reservoir access.
14. Deep Creek, tributary of the Owyhee River.
15. Slack Mountain access point.
16. Mud Flat Guard Station, and access to Triangle road.
17. Dry Creek; Battle Creek access to south, Antelope Ridge to North.
18. Juniper Station access to north.
19. Battle Creek access.
20. Perjue canyon access.
21. Shoofly creek, and Between the Creeks access.
22. Poison Creek cutoff road to Oreana.
23. Shoofly cutoff to Jacks Creek areas.

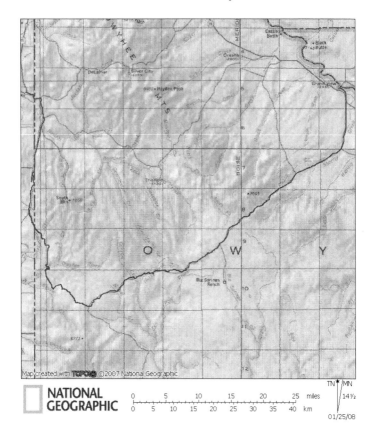

Mud Flat Rd. Overview

Juniper Mountain from the Mud Flat Road.

Area 5 Route 29 – Three Forks via Mud Flat Rd

Topo 7.5" series: Jordan Valley, OR ID, Stonehouse
  Creek, ID, Parsnip Peak, OR ID, Juniper Point, OR
  ID, Brewster Reservoir, OR ID, Three Forks, OR
Grade III
Difficulty: Easy, moderate at Three Forks Dome area.
Route Start: Jordan Valley, OR
Length of route: aprox 39 miles to Three Forks of the
  Owyhee River
Starting coords: 42°58'27" N, 117°03'12" W
Finish coords: 42°31'45" N, 117°11'00" W

Route description:

42°58'27" N, 117°03'12" W
Pleasnt Valley School
42°53'58" N, 117°00'14" W
→ 42°41'58" N, 117°02'09" W
↑ 42°40'48" N, 117°04'20" W
↑ 42°39'05" N, 117°05'40" W
← 42°35'04" N, 117°07'48" W
→ 42°34'53" N, 117°07'31" W
↑ 42°34'29" N, 117°07'39" W
Canyon Rim
42°33'19" N, 117°09'16" W
Three Forks of the Owyhee River
42°32'39" N, 117°09'47" W

North Fork crossing
42°32'33" N, 117°09'31" W
→ 42°31'56" N, 117°09'47" W
Owyhee River hot springs
42°31'45" N, 117°11'00" W

Three Forks is a popular destination with river runners and campers alike. There are two access points, Mud Flat, or Highway 95. The road descending to the river is rough, steep and should not be attempted in slick conditions. There are some primitive campsites and toilet facilities available at the river. After fording the North Fork, you can traverse past Three Forks Dome and take a rough road down to the river. There are a few hot springs along the road cut, and across the river is Warm Springs Canyon, an incredible creek that is entirely made up of hot water. There are two phenomenal pools to soak in but both require a fording of the Owyhee River. Needless to say, it can only be attempted during low water flows. There is another access via Rome, which allows travel on the opposite side of the river, and I will include that as another route. While looking at the opposite bank, and the hot spring area, note the road built by the early stage line as access to the crossing of the Owyhee. BLM signs are posted at Highway 95 and at a few of the other road junctions on the way to Three Forks. No water is available. Three Forks was a popular location with the

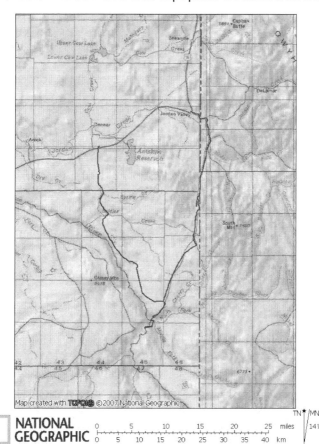

Indians, and was used as a location for Camp Three Forks, a military installation from around 1866 through the Snake War and finally was abandoned in 1871 and the land sold and turned into a cattle ranch. One old story has the cavalry hauling a cannon across the river when attacked by a band of Indians. Legend has it that the cannon was sent to the bottom of the river and wasn't raised until many years later. The road that is built around the Warm Springs Canyon area is an incredible display of rockwork and well worth exploring. Called the "W" grade, it was built except for the last hundred feet or so. Stagecoaches and wagons were lowered over the edge with ropes.

Three Forks of the Owyhee River via Jordan Valley and US Highway 95

Area 4 Route 30 – Three Forks via Highway 95

Topo 7.5" series: Jordan Valley, OR ID, Antelope Reservoir, OR, Danner, OR, Little Grassy Mountain, OR, Skull Creek, OR, Whitehorse Butte, OR, Three Forks, OR
Grade III
Difficulty: Easy, moderate at Three Forks Dome area.
Route Start: Jordan Valley, OR
Length of route: aprox 41 miles to Three Forks of the Owyhee River
Starting coords: 42°54'15" N, 117°18'56" W
Finish coords: 42°31'45" N, 117°11'00" W

Route description:

42°54'15" N, 117°18'56" W
↑ 42°49'25" N, 117°18'58" W
→ 42°48'17" N, 117°18'16" W
↑ 42°47'39" N, 117°18'43" W
→ 42°45'46" N, 117°17'24" W
Owyhee Canyon Overlook
42°41'28" N, 117°16'09" W
→ 42°35'04" N, 117°07'48" W
→ 42°34'53" N, 117°07'31" W
Canyon Rim Overlook
42°33'19" N, 117°09'16" W
Three Forks of the Owyhee River
42°32'39" N, 117°09'47" W

North Fork crossing
42°32'33" N, 117°09'31" W
→ 42°31'56" N, 117°09'47" W
Owyhee River hot springs
42°31'45" N, 117°11'00" W

Area 4 Route 31 – Rome to Three Forks

Topo 7.5" series: Jordan Valley, OR ID, Antelope Res-
  ervoir, OR, Danner, OR, Little Grassy Mountain,
  OR, Skull Creek, OR, Whitehorse Butte, OR, Three
  Forks, OR
Grade IV
Difficulty: Moderate due to length and route finding
Route Start: Rome, OR
Length of route: aprox 37 miles to Three Forks of the
  Owyhee River
Starting coords: 42°50'15" N, 117°37'56" W
Finish coords: 42°31'39" N, 117°10'59" W

Route description:

42°50'15" N, 117°37'56" W
← 42°49'05" N, 117°37'16" W
← 42°48'27" N, 117°36'55" W
← 42°47'41" N, 117°36'16" W
← 42°47'00" N, 117°35'36" W
↑ 42°46'23" N, 117°32'18" W
← 42°45'30" N, 117°29'37" W
↑ 42°41'52" N, 117°20'31" W
↑ 42°41'34" N, 117°19'53" W
← 42°41'17" N, 117°19'26" W
→ 42°38'13" N, 117°17'32" W
← 42°36'46" N, 117°16'07" W
← 42°35'23" N, 117°15'21" W
→ 42°34'43" N, 117°14'51" W
← 42°31'54" N, 117°12'51" W
42°31'39" N, 117°10'59" W

The small town of Rome Oregon sits at the historical "Crossing of the Owyhee" and was a major point on the Emigrant Trail. In early times, the Owyhee River was the state line between Oregon and Idaho. Ancient man has been crossing the Owyhee River for over 10,000 years.

Trapping parties have left diaries that show the river was being trapped as early as 1812 by Hudson Bay Company men. The original name of the Owyhee was the Sandwich Island River, based on the early name of Hawaii. In 1819 natives killed three Sandwich Island natives, and the river took on the phonetic sound of Hawaii, and its current sound and name.

The crossing was named Rome in 1919, and was named after the incredible geological formations that surrounded the river. Their columnar striations and colors were said to look like the ruined temples of Rome. It is well documented that the towering cliffs are quite incredible. Upstream at the headwaters of Bogus Creek are the fantastic China Gardens, an incredible array of twisted and colorful sculpted rock formations. This route can be deceiving, but if you continue to keep close to the canyon you will not have any prob-

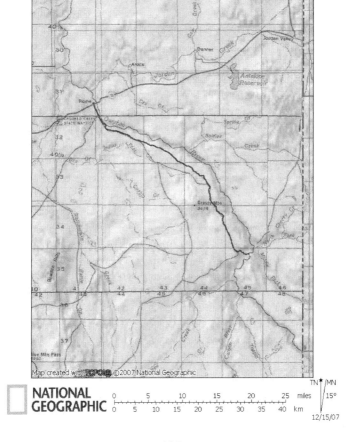

lems. It goes without saying that as you head south from Rome you are truly flying without much of a net. Make sure your route is known by someone other than yourself, and that all of your mechanical items are in good working order. You are on your own.

Area 5 Route 32 – North Fork Owyhee River

Topo 7.5" series: Jordan Valley, OR ID, Parsnip Peak, OR ID, Juniper Point, OR ID, Cliffs, ID, Fairylawn, ID
Grade III
Difficulty: Easy with great early season camping.
Route Start: Jordan Valley, OR
Length of route: aprox 32 miles to North Fork camp-ground
Starting coords: 42°58'27" N, 117°03'12" W
Finish coords: 42°35'31" N, 116°58'53" W

Route description:

42°58'27" N, 117°03'12" W
Jordan Creek
42°54'48" N, 116°59'42" W
Pleasnt Valley School
42°53'58" N, 117°00'14" W
← 42°41'57" N, 117°02'08" W
Dougal Resevoir and Ranch
42°39'26" N, 117°00'11" W
Cliffs road access
42°38'21" N, 116°58'52" W
North Fork overlook and view
42°35'49" N, 116°59'23" W
North Fork Campground

42°35'31" N, 116°58'53" W

The North Fork of the Owyhee is a jagged canyon cut into the flat tableland of the desert. With little or no warning it opens up before you as you climb up from Cliffs. The spectacular hoodoos and spires take your breath away as you ride down the steep grade and into the BLM primitive campground area. A toilet and several sites with tables are all that awaits you. Upstream is a short hike to an old homestead cabin and corrals. Be aware of snakes during the warmer season. They are usually more afraid of you than the other way around.

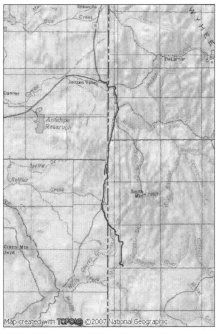

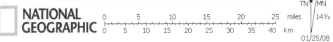

Past the North Fork the road climbs steeply up and out and there is good short trips upstream on the left (42°35'23" N, 116°59'12" W). Fairylawn (42°34'10" N, 116°59'21" W), and the Squaw Creek Vee (42°33'27" N, 116°58'32" W) follow farther, and finally you can loop all the way over to Three Forks via the Circle Bar Ranch at 42°33'03" N, 116°58'22" W

Looking down into the Incredible North Fork of the Owyhee River Canyon. The BLM campground is to the left of the bridge.

Area 5 Route 33 – Red Canyon

Topo 7.5" series: Jordan Valley, OR ID, Parsnip Peak,
   OR ID, Juniper Point, OR ID, Cliffs, ID, Fairylawn,
   ID, Bedstead Ridge, ID, Smith Creek, ID, Red Basin,
   ID
Grade IV
Difficulty: Difficult, due to length and remoteness.
Route Start: Jordan Valley, OR
Length of route: aprox 66 miles to Red Canyon.
Starting coords: 42°58'27" N, 117°03'12" W
Finish coords: 42°18'05" N, 116°51'16" W

Route description:

42°58'27" N, 117°03'12" W
Pleasnt Valley School
42°53'58" N, 117°00'14" W
Dougal Resevoir and Ranch
42°39'26" N, 117°00'11" W
North Fork Campground
42°35'31" N, 116°58'53" W
→ 42°31'02" N, 116°53'38" W
← 42°30'55" N, 116°53'37" W
Payne Cabin
42°29'38" N, 116°53'17" W
← 42°26'44" N, 116°52'32" W
← 42°26'36" N, 116°51'58" W
→ 42°26'30" N, 116°51'23" W
→ 42°25'04" N, 116°48'47" W
→ 42°22'42" N, 116°48'26" W
← 42°20'16" N, 116°50'17" W
* → **Bull Basin access**
→ 42°19'36" N, 116°50'25" W
* ← **Defeat Ridge/Lambert Table**

Red Canyon
42°18'05" N, 116°51'16" W

Red Canyon is a spectacular ride in the Owyhee Canyonlands area. It is lengthy, moderately difficult, and
historically interesting. Another foray into the Juniper
Mountain Breaks area off the back of the infamous Juniper Mountain. The ride weaves its way along ridge-
lines until finally diving into the canyon and arrives
close to the Owyhee River. A few different routes can
either link up with Lambert Table, Brace Flat and the

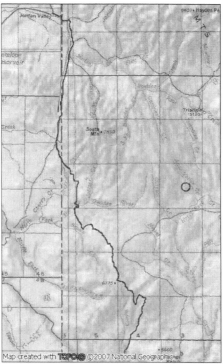

Brace Ranch, or Bull Basin, the notorious location of convicted outlaw Claude Dallas.

This is about as far as a human can get from pavement in the lower United States. You should plan accordingly. A fifty-mile walk out is not an easy undertaking in the event of a serious breakdown or accident.

The Lambert Table is reached via Defeat Ridge, and can be crossed and linked back up to return via the Star Ranch route, or by heading through Red Canyon, Bull Basin and back to your original starting point. More than likely all you will see here is wildlife, including Desert Bighorn and Pronghorn Antelope.

Rickard's Crossing of the Owyhee River.
One of the most remote sections of
real estate in the entire lower 48.

I did an overnight tour here in May of 2007, and spent the night at Rattlesnake Springs, on my way to looping the Lambert Table. In July a lightning caused fire burned hundreds of thousands of acres, and I am not entirely sure what damage has been incurred. The aerial photos show an immense area blackened by the blaze. There will be a serious effort to re-seed and to prohibit erosion of the fragile areas. Double check all access hopes with the local jurisdictions, and heed their regulations and restrictions. We can only hope that the land will recover quickly.

Area 5 Route 34 – Bull Basin
– Crutcher's Crossing

Topo 7.5" series: Jordan Valley, OR ID, Parsnip Peak, OR ID, Juniper Point, OR ID, Cliffs, ID, Fairylawn, ID, Smith Creek, ID, Bedstead Ridge, ID, Bull Basin Camp, ID, Red Basin, ID
Grade IV
Difficulty: Difficult, due to length and remoteness.
Route Start: Jordan Valley, OR
Length of route: aprox 66 miles to Crutcher's Crossing
Starting coords: 42°58'27" N, 117°03'12" W
Finish coords: 42°18'05" N, 116°51'16" W

Route description:

42°58'27" N, 117°03'12" W
Pleasnt Valley School
42°53'58" N, 117°00'14" W
Dougal Resevoir and Ranch
42°39'26" N, 117°00'11" W

North Fork Campground
42°35'31" N, 116°58'53" W
→ 42°31'02" N, 116°53'38" W
← 42°30'55" N, 116°53'37" W
Payne Cabin
42°29'38" N, 116°53'17" W
→ 42°26'46" N, 116°52'34" W
← 42°26'39" N, 116°52'40" W
← 42°26'06" N, 116°52'45" W
← 42°22'54" N, 116°55'47" W
→ 42°20'38" N, 116°54'19" W
* ← **Red Canyon/Lambert Table**
← 42°20'29" N, 116°54'22" W
Bull Basin Camp
42°20'26" N, 116°54'20" W
↑ 42°19'17" N, 116°53'43" W
← 42°18'43" N, 116°54'00" W
← 42°17'33" N, 116°53'02" W
42°15'36" N, 116°52'13" W

Bull Basin is the infamous location where Claude Dallas had his showdown with two Idaho Fish and Game Officers. In a Wild West type of show down, gunshot wounds killed both officers, and Dallas became the object of a nation wide manhunt. Finally caught near the Nevada border, Dallas had led authorities on a highly publicized chase. Bull basin is another location where old time horse and cattle thieves used to hold their livestock on the way back to Idaho. Crutcher's Crossing of the Owyhee is an additional 7 miles or so past Bull Basin Camp.

One of the few locations that provided access into the canyons, and then over the Owyhee River, the crossing is filled with stories of Indian raiding parties, buffalo hunts, cattle drives, horse stealing parties, and a few drownings. Today it is used by river rafters, hunters, and those of us who like to poke around the lonely desert locales. The remoteness of this trip reminds us again of the ability to be completely self reliant, both mechanically and physically. No services or help will be encountered for many miles. This portion of the Owyhee exemplifies the name "Big Quiet".

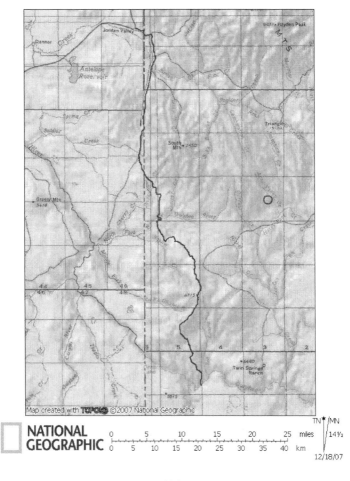

Rumor has it that the old wooden structures at Crutchers were lost in the wildfire of 2007. This fire underscores the delicate conditions that the desert can quickly become. Always be extremely careful with any use of fire, and make sure your exhaust system meets or exceeds all required Forest Service requirements for spark arrest. Stay on trails and roads, and keep your hot engine parts away from any combustible brush or grasses that might be near your path. Fire suppression is far away and very limited.

Area 5 Route 35 – Upper & Lower Battle Creek

Topo 7.5" series: Grand View, ID, Chalk Hills, ID, Purjue Canyon, ID, Rough Mountain, ID, Snow Creek, ID, Clover Mountain, ID, Big Springs Ranch, ID, Crab Spring Butte, ID, Lost Valley, ID, Turner Table, ID, Nichol Flat, ID, Flying H Ranch, ID, Riddle, ID
Grade IV
Difficulty: Difficult, rocky, remote, long and difficult route finding.
Route Start: Grandview, ID
Length of route: aprox 82 miles to Riddle, ID.
Starting coords: 42°59'00" N, 116°05'51" W
Finish coords: 42°11'13" N, 116°06'38" W

Route description: Dry Cr./Upper Battle

42°59'00" N, 116°05'51" W
← 42°39'46" N, 116°26'27" W
↑ 42°39'17" N, 116°26'31" W
→ 42°37'58" N, 116°26'24" W
← 42°37'19" N, 116°26'48" W
← 42°36'42" N, 116°26'32" W

↑ 42°35'54" N, 116°25'14" W
↑ 42°35'23" N, 116°25'01" W
← 42°33'35" N, 116°23'13" W
→ 42°32'47" N, 116°21'08" W
→ 42°31'50" N, 116°20'45" W
← 42°31'30" N, 116°20'59" W
Upper Battle Creek Crossing
42°28'40" N, 116°19'23" W
← 42°27'34" N, 116°18'00" W
→ 42°27'42" N, 116°16'49" W
→ 42°24'41" N, 116°14'49" W
← 42°23'27" N, 116°15'27" W
→ 42°19'49" N, 116°14'23" W
← 42°17'57" N, 116°12'25" W
← 42°17'56" N, 116°12'16" W
→ 42°18'23" N, 116°11'02" W
→ 42°15'36" N, 116°08'50" W
← 42°13'35" N, 116°10'35" W
→ 42°12'22" N, 116°06'34" W
42°11'13" N, 116°06'38" W

Lower Battle Creek at Mud Flat Rd:

← 42°41'27" N, 116°24'23" W
← 42°39'48" N, 116°21'51" W
→ 42°40'11" N, 116°21'41" W
→ 42°39'40" N, 116°20'32" W
↑ 42°39'27" N, 116°20'24" W
→ 42°39'15" N, 116°19'57" W
← 42°38'13" N, 116°19'29" W
← 42°37'50" N, 116°18'01" W
← 42°37'15" N, 116°17'43" W
→ 42°33'54" N, 116°17'40" W
← 42°33'03" N, 116°20'32" W
← 42°32'47" N, 116°21'08" W
Rejoins overall route here

Battle Creek is a long and very remote ride that takes you almost directly south through the heart of the steppes. It is filled with grand sweeping vistas, rocky trails, hidden reservoirs, and lonely ranches. Start either at the lower Battle Creek crossing area or at Dry Creek, both reached via the Mud Flat road. Heading south you will wind your way past multiple roads and vague trails. Route finding is somewhat tricky, but all trails seem to eventually make their way back to the main route. I remember only having to back track 3 or 4 times! There are petroglyphs marked at 42°31'10" N, 116°21'42" W, but I have not visited them. Big remote

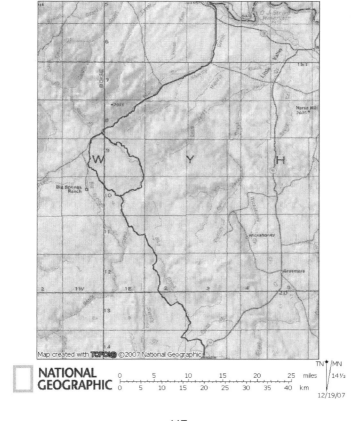

NATIONAL
GEOGRAPHIC

Map created with TOPO!® ©2007 National Geographic

| 0 | 5 | 10 | 15 | 20 | 25 | miles |
| 0 | 5 | 10 | 15 | 20 | 25 | 30 | 35 | 40 | km |

TN / MN
14½

12/19/07

ranches are the norm here, and multi generation families continue to operate a special lifestyle that only this big country can support. Lower Battle Creek follows the creek for approximately 17 miles before joining up with the Blue Creek drainage. There is gas at the Duck Valley Indian Reservation.

Area 6 Route 36 – Wickahoney & Grasmere

Topo 7.5" series: Bruneau, ID, Sugar Valley, ID, Hot Spring, ID, Broken Wagon Flat, ID, Table Butte, ID, Wickahoney Crossing, ID, Hill Pasture, ID, Grasmere, ID, Grasmere Reservoir, ID

Grade IV

Difficulty: Difficult with rocky, remote and multiple trails.

Route Start: Bruneau, ID

Length of route: aprox 52 miles to Grasmere, ID.

Starting coords: 42°52'51" N, 115°47'48" W

Finish coords: 42°11'13" N, 116°06'38" W

Route description:

42°52'51" N, 115°47'48" W

→ 42°47'30" N, 115°43'06" W

← 42°47'35" N, 115°43'46" W

→ 42°45'27" N, 115°45'12" W

* ← Indian Bathtubs/Bruneau Hot Sprg.

→ 42°43'33" N, 115°45'50" W CCC Rd.

* ← Blackstone/Grasmere Road

← 42°38'59" N, 115°47'31" W

Junction w Highway 51

↑ 42°33'10" N, 115°53'52" W

← 42°33'18" N, 115°56'34" W

← 42°33'22" N, 115°58'57" W
Wickahoney Crossing
42°32'32" N, 115°58'41" W
← 42°31'49" N, 115°58'54" W
← 42°31'45" N, 115°58'55" W
→ 42°31'05" N, 115°58'54" W
Wickahoney Station
42°27'22" N, 115°59'02" W
← 42°27'14" N, 115°58'59" W
→ 42°27'07" N, 115°58'48" W
→ 42°24'11" N, 115°57'38" W
* ← **China Creek access**
← 42°23'09" N, 115°57'22" W
↑ 42°22'34" N, 115°55'19" W
→ 42°22'57" N, 115°53'05" W Hwy 51
42°22'38" N, 115°53'05" W

Zeno Falls access:

→ 42°31'49" N, 115°58'54" W
→ 42°31'57" N, 116°00'15" W
← 42°33'08" N, 116°02'03" W
← 42°33'45" N, 116°02'39" W
* → **Holman Cabin 1 mile down canyon (Big Jacks Creek)**
← 42°30'42" N, 116°04'33" W
* → **Harvey Place 42°30'45" N, 116°04'41" W**
42°30'23" N, 116°04'11" W Hicks Springs and Zeno Canyon access

The ruins of the Wickahoney Station still remain out on the Owyhee plain. A stage stop and functioning post office, the ranch was settled in 1887, the stone structure started in 1895, and was used until around 1930 when the route from Mountain City, Nevada, and Mountain Home, Idaho was changed. The lush Wickahoney Springs watered the station. The station is listed on the register of the National Historical Places. Nearby is the remote Zeno Falls. This side route circles around Duncan Creek Canyon and ends near Hicks Springs. A difficult hike down into the canyon will bring you to one of the Owyhee Deserts most famous waterfalls. Many riders will start at Highway 51, but to add even more adventure, begin in Bruneau and take the Grasmere and CCC Road across the desert. An alternate path down China Creek is available close to the end of the ride and travels by the Sego Place.

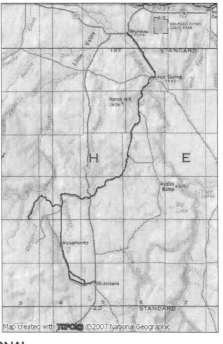

Area 6 Route 37 – Bruneau Desert

Topo 7.5" series: Bruneau, ID, Sugar Valley, ID, Hot
  Spring, ID, Crowbar Gulch, ID, Pot Hole Butte, ID,
  Winter Camp, ID, Hodge Station, ID, Juniper Ranch,
  ID, Clover Butte North, ID, Juniper Butte, ID, Mos-
  quito Lake Butte, ID, Murphy Hot Springs, ID,
Grade IV
Difficulty: Moderate due to length of trail and remote-
  ness.
Route Start: Bruneau, ID
Length of route: aprox 77 miles to Murphy Hot
  Springs
Starting coords: 42°52'51" N, 115°47'48" W
Finish coords: 42°01'34" N, 115°21'42" W

Route description:

42°52'51" N, 115°47'48" W
← 42°47'30" N, 115°43'05" W
← 42°47'04" N, 115°42'50" W
→ 42°45'27" N, 115°39'37" W
↑ 42°44'25" N, 115°38'52" W
Bruneau Overlook turn junction
42°42'36" N, 115°37'19" W
→ 42°29'02" N, 115°22'46" W
Clover Creek crossing
42°26'57" N, 115°22'30" W
← 42°07'35" N, 115°18'09" W
→ 42°04'54" N, 115°15'05" W
Nevada (border) junction (2 miles)
42°00'38" N, 115°20'15" W
Murphy Hot Spring
42°01'34" N, 115°21'42" W

Get Lost! Adventure Tours in the Owyhee Desert

The Bruneau Desert is a wide-open expanse that everyone needs to experience on a bike. The road runs from the little hamlet of Bruneau, and then heads out across the desert and the Air Force bombing range.

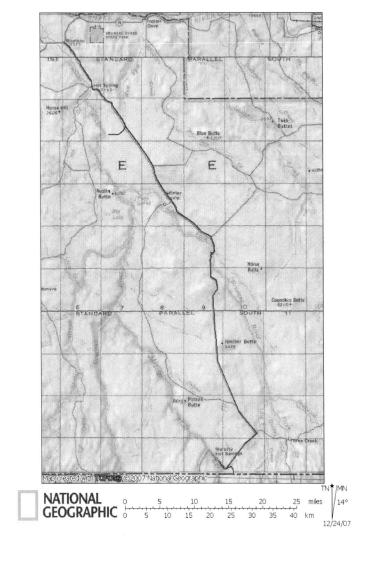

The overlook of the Bruneau Canyon is truly magnificent, and can't be missed. This ride is a classic, traveling to the Nevada border area and the old town of Murphy's Hot Springs. In early times, the site was owned by the Wilkins Family, and Kittie Wilkins, called by most "the Horse Queen of Idaho" built a well-known stock raising ranch in the area. The hot springs are private, but have been well known for hundreds of years. The early pioneers named it the Hot Hole. If you continue down and to the fork of the Jarbidge River, you can travel to Jarbidge proper. This will be the only gas available so check locally before taking off across the desert!

The Bruneau Desert. A true open space

Area 6 Route 38 – Idaho Centennial Trail

Topo 7.5" series: Bruneau, ID, Sugar Valley, ID, Hot
Spring, ID, Crowbar Gulch, ID, Pot Hole Butte, ID,
Winter Camp, ID, Hodge Station, ID, Juniper Ranch,
ID, Clover Butte North, ID, Juniper Butte, ID, Mos-
quito Lake Butte, ID, Murphy Hot Springs, ID,
Grade IV- V
Difficulty: Moderate with remote and multiple long
mileage legs.
Route Start: Idaho, Nevada border.
Length of route: aprox 91 miles to Hammett, ID Round
trip as high as 200 miles
Starting coords: 42°00'00" N, 115°19'09" W
Finish coords: 42°01'34" N, 115°21'42" W

Route description:

Nevada Border
42°00'00" N, 115°19'09" W
↑ 42°00'36" N, 115°20'15" W
← 42°02'46" N, 115°22'05" W
→ 42°07'48" N, 115°26'51" W
← 42°08'29" N, 115°25'03" W
← 42°09'29" N, 115°24'34" W
← 42°14'36" N, 115°30'13" W
→ 42°15'16" N, 115°31'39" W
→ 42°21'24" N, 115°35'06" W
Bengoeachea Cabin
42°23'31" N, 115°34'45" W
→ 42°24'22" N, 115°34'32" W
← 42°25'01" N, 115°34'16" W
→ 42°27'19" N, 115°34'24" W
→ 42°31'14" N, 115°33'18" W
← 42°33'40" N, 115°30'22" W

← 42°38'15" N, 115°39'01" W
→ 42°38'15" N, 115°39'01" W
← 42°41'32" N, 115°38'50" W
→ 42°45'27" N, 115°39'37" W
← 42°45'36" N, 115°39'23" W
→ 42°48'33" N, 115°38'07" W
← 42°53'41" N, 115°33'33" W
→ 42°56'00" N, 115°33'32" W
Hammett
42°56'45" N, 115°27'58" W

Route description: Bruneau Desert main route

42°52'51" N, 115°47'48" W
← 42°47'30" N, 115°43'05" W
← 42°47'04" N, 115°42'50" W
→ 42°45'27" N, 115°39'37" W
↑ 42°44'25" N, 115°38'52" W
Bruneau Overlook turn junction
42°42'36" N, 115°37'19" W
→ 42°29'02" N, 115°22'46" W
Clover Creek crossing
42°26'57" N, 115°22'30" W
← 42°07'35" N, 115°18'09" W
→ 42°04'54" N, 115°15'05" W
Nevada (border) junction
42°00'38" N, 115°20'15" W
Murphy Hot Spring
42°01'34" N, 115°21'42" W

This Idaho Centennial Trail section is the first section from the Nevada border, to the small rural town
of Hammett. The easiest way to do this section is to
probably take the Bruneau Desert ride as described
in Route #38. Continue on to Jarbidge, NV. After fuel-

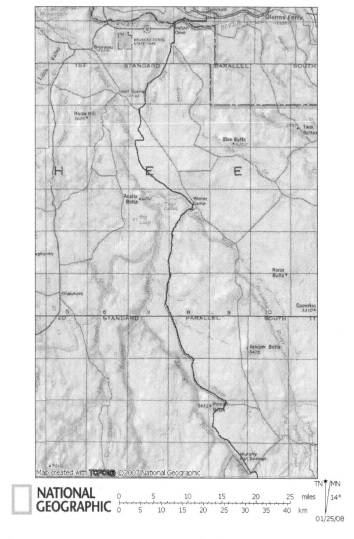

Map created with TOPO! ©2007 National Geographic

NATIONAL GEOGRAPHIC

TN ↑ MN

0	5	10	15	20	25	miles
0	5	10	15	20	25	30	35	40	km

14°

01/25/08

ing up, retrace your steps to the border junction and then go from there. Round trip it's probably close to 200 miles. Winter Camp and the Clover Creek areas are both beautifully subtle in their relief from the stark areas. Water is precious in the desert! The route generally follows as close to the Bruneau Canyon as feasible with a swing over to the East as you close in on the Snake River. Finishing at Hammett, one can return to most destinations for a really nice loop. There are a few very cool campsites at the creeks, and this would be a really fun and easy weekend tour.

Area 1 Route 39 – Vale to Rome

Topo 7.5" series: Vale West, OR, Double Mountain, OR, Kane Spring Gulch, OR, Sourdough Spring, OR, Twin Springs, OR, Quartz Mountain Basin, OR, Diamond Butte, OR, Big Mud Flat, OR, The Hole in the Ground, OR, Rinehart Canyon, OR, Sacramento Butte, OR, Wrangle Butte, OR, Lambert Rocks, OR, Iron Mountain, OR, Owyhee Butte, OR, Rome, OR
Grade IV- V
Difficulty: Difficult with remote route finding and long mileage.
Route Start: Vale Or.
Length of route: aprox 130 miles to Rome OR.
Starting coords: 43°58'57" N, 117°14'16" W
Finish coords: 42°50'20" N, 117°37'42" W

Route description:

43°58'57" N, 117°14'16" W
Vale Oregon, continue West on US Hwy 20
← 43°56'16" N, 117°22'32" W (Bishop Rd)
→ 43°55'14" N, 117°22'31" W (Rock Canyon Rd)
→ 43°52'42" N, 117°21'57" W
←43°42'25" N, 117°23'51" W (Twin Springs Rd)
→ 43°41'41" N, 117°23'36" W
→ 43°36'57" N, 117°25'04" W (Dry Cr Rd)

→ 43°36'02" N, 117°24'36" W
→ 43°34'16" N, 117°24'39" W
← 43°29'28" N, 117°27'21" W
→ 43°29'09" N, 117°27'15" W
→ 43°26'41" N, 117°27'06" W
← 43°26'50" N, 117°27'28" W
→ 43°24'19" N, 117°26'29" W
→ 43°20'02" N, 117°27'38" W
→ 43°15'33" N, 117°29'58" W
→ 43°15'21" N, 117°31'30" W
← 43°16'55" N, 117°31'40" W
← 43°16'45" N, 117°36'33" W (Turner Rd)
→ 43°15'13" N, 117°37'09" W
← 43°14'21" N, 117°40'11" W
→ 43°13'18" N, 117°40'04" W (Rinehart Ranch Rd)
← 43°13'41" N, 117°43'26" W
↑ 43°08'08" N, 117°47'35" W (Tub Springs Rd)
↑ 43°05'23" N, 117°47'35" W
→ 43°00'51" N, 117°45'59" W
↑ 42°53'02" N, 117°45'13" W (Kiger Rd)
→ 42°51'32" N, 117°43'38" W
← 42°50'48" N, 117°42'56" W
→ 42°51'36" N, 117°39'10" W (Old ION Hwy)
← 42°51'22" N, 117°39'17" W
42°50'20" N, 117°37'42" W Rome OR

The west side of the Owyhee Reservoir is truly a lone-some area. This ride is very lengthy, is rarely traveled, and is rich in wildlife and geological topography. I tried a couple of times to link this route, but unfortunately ran out of time both times. I have only talked to one individual who had ridden to Rome from Vale, and I didn't get his specific route, as even he wasn't sure of it! Needless to say this route is a big undertaking with long distance and remote route finding necessary for success. There are a myriad of offshoots that access interesting named areas along the Owyhee River. Ranch sites and stock ponds, springs, lava rock and mountain vistas are all out here. The route offers a chance for a multi-day tour or a really long day ride for the true warrior.

This ride ranks high on my to do list. I look forward to hearing from others as to what they find!

Chapter 9

Government and Land Owners

While traveling in the backcountry, you will come across a few items that are generally repetitive to the landscape. Here are some basic guidelines to follow when encountering them.

Gates crisscross the Owyhee desert, and the basic protocol is to leave all gates as you find them. If the gate is open, then leave it open. If it is closed, be sure to close and secure it properly as you pass through. Owyhee cattlemen use a leverage style of bar to help keep the gate tight and straight. It will take a bit of practice to get the hang of it, but don't worry you'll get it!

Cattle are the life and blood of the vast acreage that makes up our BLM land. You must SLOW down as you approach and pass cattle. It is especially important to not push the cattle into a run, or to separate the young calves from their mothers. Keep your speed, noise, and dust to a minimum. These animals are the ranchers' lifeblood! Respect them and do everything you can to not disturb their animals.

Ask before you use, or trespass on private lands. It is your responsibility to find out who owns the land you are hoping to access. Be proactive and ask county employees, Sheriffs, local business/store owners, gas station attendants, Game Wardens, and anyone who might be able to give you information on land ownership. Don't be afraid to walk up and knock on doors. Be real, and be open! Thank you notes are always a nice touch, as are reports of anything unusual that you might have seen during your travels. Ask if there is anything you can do if you are in the area. Many ranch families are far from town, and could be helped by simply bringing an item from town and thus saving them time and effort. Ask how you can help! It can only make your future access that much more acceptable.

Travel corridors exist and when using these you must stick to the road or trail, and do not trespass outside of the corridor. By allowing access through their lands, owners are being gracious and hospitable. Don't betray their trust. Homesites, cabins, and other historical items are usually located on private property. They are an incredible opportunity to have a glimpse into the past. Many are in almost pristine condition, and some are still being used to this day. Do not damage, or vandalize any of these locations. Remember, take only pictures, and leave only footprints, or in this case, single tracks!

It should go without saying that you should never litter or leave trash or other items that would mar the landscape. Be a good steward and leave the desert better than when you arrived. Better yet, join a local riding club and participate in some of the local clean up efforts. Not only will you meet and learn a tremendous amount about areas to ride in; you will also help to develop lasting relationships with State and Federal agencies that work in these same areas. Without communication and relationships with these folks at the local level, we stand to lose many rights and areas to closures.

Local Contact information:

BLM Vale office
100 Oregon St.
Vale OR 97918
541-473-3144

BLM Marsing office
20 First Ave. West
Marsing, ID 83639
208-896-5912

BLM Bruneau office
3948 Development Ave
Boise, ID 83105
208-384-3300

BLM Jarbidge office (Twin Falls District)
2536 Kimberly Rd
Twin Falls, ID 83301
208-736-2350

Owyhee Historical Society
Museum Hours: Tue - Sat 10:00 a.m. to 4:00 p.m.
Library and Research Center by appointment only
17085 Basey St
PO Box 67
Murphy, ID 83650
(208) 495-2319
(208) 495-9824 Fax

Chapter 10

Appendices

The following books were essential in providing research, information, history and other critical data in preparing this guidebook. They are all recommended reading if you are interested in learning about the Owyhee country.

Roadside Geology of Idaho
David D. Alt
Mountain Press Publishing Com-
    pany, Missoula MT 1989

Idaho A Climbing Guide
Tom Lopez
The Mountaineers, Seattle WA 2000

Guide to the Geology of the Owyhee Re-
    gion of Oregon Bulletin #21
University of Oregon, Eugene OR 1973

Exploring Idaho's High Desert
Sheldon Bluestein
www.hike.idaho.com

In Times Past, A History of the Low-
    er Jordan Creek Communities
Hazel R. Fretwell-Johnson
The Print Shoppe, Filer ID 1990

Owyhee Graffiti Volume 1
Michael Hanley IV
Owyhee Publishing Co., Inc. Homedale ID

Idaho Place Names, A Geographical Dictionary
Lalia Boone
The University of Idaho Press, Moscow ID 1998

Sagebrush Country, A Wildflower Sanctuary
Ronald J. Taylor
Mountain Press Publishing Com-
   pany, Missoula MT 1992

Owyhee Cattlemen, 1878 – 1978
   100 Years in the Saddle
Mildretta Adams
Owyhee Publishing Co., Inc. Homedale ID 1979

Historic Silver City, the Story of the Owyhees
Mildretta Adams
Owyhee Publishing Co., Inc. Homedale ID 1969

To purchase additional copies
of the *Get Lost* guidebook, go to

www.getlostoffroad.com.